Through the Communication Barrier

S. I. HAYAKAWA

United States Senate

THROUGH THE COMMUNICATION BARRIER

On Speaking, Listening, and Understanding

Edited by
Arthur Chandler
San Francisco State University

Harper & Row, Publishers

New York, Hagerstown, San Francisco, London

Respectfully dedicated to
the memory of Alfred Korzybski
(1879–1950)

"It Helps to Be Listened To" originally appeared as "The Task of the Listener"
in *"ETC."* "The Language of Social Disagreement" originally appeared as "Semantics, Law, and Priestly Minded Men" in *Western Reserve Law Review.*

Copyright acknowledgments appear on page 169.

THROUGH THE COMMUNICATION BARRIER. Copyright © 1979 by S. I. Hayakawa.
All rights reserved. Printed in the United States of America. No part of this
book may be used or reproduced in any manner whatsoever without written
permission except in the case of brief quotations embodied in critical articles
and reviews. For information address Harper & Row, Publishers, Inc., 10 East
53rd Street, New York, N.Y. 10022. Published simultaneously in Canada by
Fitzhenry & Whiteside Limited, Toronto.

FIRST EDITION

Designed by Janice Stern

Library of Congress Cataloging in Publication Data
Hayakawa, Samuel Ichiyé, 1906–
    Through the communication barrier.
    1. Communication—Addresses, essays, lectures.
    2. Semantics—Addresses, essays, lectures.
    I. Title.
P91.25.H33 1979   001.5   75-30332
ISBN 0–06–011791–5

79 80 81 82 83 10 9

P
91.25
.H33
1979

Hayakawa, S. I.

Through the
    communication barrier

001.5 H323t

CONTENTS

PART VII: The Language of Social Agreement

Acknowledgments

I am deeply indebted to Professor Arthur Chandler of San Francisco State University and to Amy Bonoff of Harper & Row for editorial assistance and helpful suggestions in the preparation of this volume.

Introduction

I first met Alfred Korzybski (1879–1950), the founder of the school of thought known as "general semantics," in September 1938, when he invited me to one of his seminars in Chicago. I was at the time a circuit-riding instructor in the University of Wisconsin Extension Division, teaching freshman English in little cities like Wausau, Rhinelander, Manitowoc, and Antigo.

At the time and for many years thereafter my great desire as a teacher was to teach young people to write well, which of course means thinking clearly. Finding my students given to parroting the clichés of radio newscasters and patent-medicine commercials in their speaking and writing, I was very much in search of an intellectual discipline that would sharpen their critical awareness of language.

There were political as well as pedagogical reasons for being interested in semantics at that time. Like many others of the decade of the 1930s, I watched with alarm the rise of fascism in Europe and feared the possibility of similar developments in America. It seemed to many of us then that political propaganda had become, as the result of radio, more powerful and penetrating and persuasive than ever before in world history. Europe had Hitler and Mussolini—powerful propagandists. In America we also had gifted radio orators who were seen by many as potential fascist threats. Some feared Huey Long; others feared Father Coughlin; the Liberty League feared Franklin D. Roosevelt, whose eloquence on radio was the envy and despair of his political opponents. To me, it seemed that if large numbers of people could be influenced by a commercial that said "Serutan: If you spell it backwards, it spells Nature's," they could be made to believe just about anything!

Liberals and conservatives alike were therefore worried in those prewar days about the dangers of propaganda. In 1936 Sinclair Lewis dramatized his fears in his novel *It Can't Happen Here.* The Institute of Propaganda Analysis was started at Teachers College of Columbia University in 1937 to produce lesson plans and teaching aids to help the student "detect propaganda" and identify the most common "propaganda devices," such as the "glittering generality," the "bandwagon effect," and the "plain folks" appeal. Stuart Chase's *The Tyranny of Words* of 1938 did much to make the general public aware of empty abstractions and other pitfalls of language; he, more than anyone else, popularized the term "semantics."

I had spent the summer of 1938 at the University of Michigan, attracted by an announcement in the summer session catalog of a course in semantics. Taught by the linguistic scholar Thomas Knott, it turned out to be a seminar in lexicography. The students were put to work reading texts and writing definitions for a proposed *Dictionary of Early Modern English*—a huge, scholarly project that was to occupy the University of Michigan for many years. None of us objected to this lexicographical work, since we all wanted to become linguistic scholars. But most of us wanted also to study what *we* called semantics—the study of the influence of language on thought and behavior. We wanted to hear discussions of the pioneering work of C. K. Ogden and I. A. Richards in *The Meaning of Meaning;* we wanted to understand the "operationalism" of P. W. Bridgman; we were curious about the "general semantics" of Alfred Korzybski. So we told Professor Knott of our desires.

Professor Knott admitted at once that the kind of semantics we were talking about was entirely outside his field, but he agreed that we were entitled to a chance to discuss these matters. Then he asked the class, "Has anyone here read Korzybski?" I was rash enough to raise my hand. Said Professor Knott, "Hayakawa, why don't you give us a lecture or two on Korzybski's *Science and Sanity*—perhaps early next week?" I was aghast. I had come to Michigan to learn about Korzybski, not to explain him. But I was stuck with the job, and the following week I did the best I could.

In the course of preparing my lectures on Korzybski, I wrote to him in Chicago asking about further instruction in general semantics. That is how it happened that he invited me to a seminar. As soon as the summer session was over, I went to Chicago and called on him at his apartment on East 56th Street, where he had set up his Institute of General Semantics.

Korzybski greeted me with great cordiality. "So you are Hayakawa! You have been lecturing on general semantics at the University of Michigan and you don't know a goddam thing about it!" I couldn't take offense at this greeting. It was warmly meant—and I was certainly in no position to disagree. I laughed and he laughed and we were on good terms at once.

Korzybski's "seminars" were certainly not seminars in any accepted academic meaning of the term. They were unabashed indoctrination sessions, usually for six or more hours a day and continuing for several days. To me they were a fascinating experience, opening up all sorts of new areas of thought and speculation. Accustomed as I was to the strict observance of the jurisdictional boundaries of academic life, in which the professor of English never lectures on physics and the physicist never lectures on political science, I found it breathtaking to listen to Korzybski take all knowledge as his province, leaping freely from psychiatry and neurology to symbolic logic to quantum mechanics to the rise of fascism to the chemistry of colloids to cultural anthropology to non-Euclidean geometry to biology and back to the human nervous system. Why the human nervous system? Because that's where everything happens.

I wrote about Korzybski in introducing the present volume because so many of his fundamental ideas have helped to shape my thinking; their influence is no doubt to be detected on almost every page. Communication, said Korzybski, is the fundamental survival mechanism of the human class of life. Beyond breathing and eating, communicating is no doubt the most important thing human beings do. Human beings are a symbolic class of life. With symbols we communicate across generations and create culture. With communication we create societies. Communication is at the heart of all human relations, and failures of communication exacerbate every kind of human conflict.

The most important of all our systems of symbols is language. Our understanding of the world is shaped by how we talk about it. However, the picture of the world we create with our language is not the world itself. The picture is not the reality. The map is not the territory. But we continue to confuse maps with territories, words with realities. Meanings lie, said Korzybski (who did not like the term "meaning" and preferred to say "semantic reaction"), not in dictionaries or definitions, but in the human nervous system. If I tell you an obscene story in Swahili and you do not understand Swahili, it is not obscene; it is not even a story. Yet we almost universally hypostatize words and imagine that they have inherent properties, such as sacredness or obscenity. To escape the traps in which language is likely to ensnare us, said Korzybski, we need to have what he called an "extensional orientation"—that is to say, the habit of thinking about the realities that words stand for, and not simply about the words themselves.

So general semantics is not simply a matter of studying language, but of studying one's self and one's own reactions. Knowing the uncertain relationship between language and reality, one is habitually skeptical, especially of those things that "everyone knows." (As e. e. cummings once wrote, "Whenever men are right, they are not young.") The student of general semantics tries, therefore, constantly to be observant and open to experience. One doesn't have to be a student of general semantics to acquire this attitude. Some people manage to retain a lot of good sense in spite of their education. But most of us, befuddled by ideologies, dogmas, and conventional wisdom, need general semantics, or something like it, to escape the tyranny of words.

The essays in the present volume were written over the past two decades for learned journals, for psychological conventions, for magazines. Several were written at a time when I was giving seminars on "Problems of Communication" at San Francisco State, where we were concerned with a wide range of human interactions: child rearing, courtship, psychotherapy, teacher-pupil relationships, education, the impact of media, the interaction of races, minority psychology, and the influence of communicative habits in all these areas. Many essays in this volume—and portions of essays—appeared originally as newspaper columns distributed by the Register and Tribune Syndicate of Des Moines, Iowa. Although I am fully involved now in my tasks in the Senate, I have deliberately kept politics out of this volume, except for the concluding essay, "Mr. Hayakawa Goes to Washington." I have been a Senator only for two years; the time to write a book on political matters is still to come.

S. I. Hayakawa

Mill Valley, California
January 3, 1979

PART I
COMMUNICATING WITH CHILDREN

General Semantics and Child Rearing*

General semantics is a general theory of how to act a little more sanely by talking to oneself a little more sanely. How do we get children to be semantically well oriented and extensional and fact-minded? Much more important, how do we teach ourselves to manifest extensional attitudes in our behavior toward them?

Whenever I say "extensional," the term "fact-minded" can be used instead. The extensional meaning of a word is that which it refers to in the nonverbal world. A "glass of water" is not a verbal definition; this thing in my hand is *it*. So an extensional attitude has us looking not for *verbal* definitions but for the *events*, the *situations in the outside world*—not words—that words are about.

We live in an age that is relatively extensional about children, at least in the section of our culture that is capable of being reached by new ideas. Earlier ideas about the nature of children in our culture were highly doctrinaire and sometimes quite dogmatic.

There was the theological approach, which maintained that babies come to us full of original sin; that is, they are inhabited by nature with devilish wills that have to be broken, so that the task of bringing up a child is somehow or other to exorcise that original sin. We never quite succeed! Then there was a less theological approach—that children are formless clay. They

* In the preparation of this chapter, the writer is deeply indebted to his wife, Margedant Peters Hayakawa, with whom all the ideas here presented have been discussed and from whose unpublished paper on the same subject many paragraphs have been appropriated, sometimes with quotation marks but more often without.

just aren't anything at all until we shape them in some way or other—by wise counsel, proper restraints and advice, and so on. And if we don't keep at it all the time, they go out of shape.

Under the impact of psychological behaviorism the notion arose that the basic idea in bringing up children is conditioning— that the child should be favorably conditioned to good habits and conditioned against bad habits, and that the child will learn the right habits more readily if the conditioning is started very early. This body of doctrine led to the fashion that raged some thirty or more years ago of extremely early toilet training and rigid schedules. Babies would cry their hearts out, but if, according to the schedule, it wasn't time to feed them, they had to be let cry. The likes and dislikes the child was to carry through life were fed into him as if he were being programmed like an electronic computer.

Each of these theories represents the effort of people to develop their children according to the model of human nature they have inside their own heads. Each can be described as an activist theory, in the sense that the active doing of something *to* the child is felt to be necessary if the child is to grow up into an acceptable citizen and taxpayer. We are an activist culture; America is a fantastically energetic nation. Perhaps it is because of our energetic character that it did not occur to anyone until quite recently to ask what would happen with children if we tried to leave them alone. From the point of view of activist theories, leaving children alone represented quite a fearful ideal. What anarchy there would be! What damage to personality! Surely they would all develop into little hoodlums and savages.

Nevertheless, within our time pioneers in the study of child development have tried in various ways to leave children alone, or at least to let them determine certain things for themselves. Readers may remember the famous experiments where babies were fed only when they expressed hunger; it was called "demand feeding." There were also experiments in which investigators put dishes in front of little children, fruit and sweets and ground meat and all sorts of things, and let the children choose for themselves without someone's trying to decide what was good for them. The investigators found that instead of anarchy and indigestion and autocratic infants, there resulted healthy, happy babies with a surprisingly orderly pattern of needs and a kind of internal schedule of their own, a pattern that could be studied and described. They tried letting eight-month-old children choose their own diets, and they found that although on some days the babies would eat too much of some things, over a two-week period they would balance their diets without any worrying on the part of adults.

Then the investigators went on to the neurology and physiology and behavior of infants and children in an extremely detailed way, asking questions like: When do they wake? When do they sleep? Eat? Cry? At what age do they sit up? At what age do they walk? When do they start piling up blocks, working puzzles? When do they start playing cooperatively with other children? And so on. Gradually a vast amount of information was built up by such people as Arnold Gesell and his associates. When I say an attempt was made to see how children would develop if they were left alone, I do not mean to give the impression that anyone thinks a child can actually be left alone without parents, siblings, or society around him. This awareness of context is referred to in the title of Arnold Gesell and Frances Ilg's widely read book *Infant and Child in the Culture of Today.* What I mean is that for a variety of reasons, among which can be scientific curiosity, there has been a trend away from what I call activist theories of child rearing. It is only by knowing what children, in one area or another of their lives, will do when left alone that we discover what remains necessary to be done in addition.

For generations it has been believed that the principal job of being a parent is to issue sufficient and proper directives. The parent says, "Do this," and "Don't do that," and "Stop that," and "Keep on doing this," and so on, and continues this all day long. If children are directed often enough, the theory is, they will straighten out and fly right.

My late mother-in-law had this hortatory habit. She found it difficult to speak to my children without in some way or other making a generalization about desired behavior—that is, a directive. She was wonderful to them; but I could not help noticing this habit of talking to children in an unfailingly instructive way. Sometimes in a spirit of play I violated good table manners. Once I greatly amused my children by taking a giant mound of Jell-O and slurping it down in one gulp. The children were enormously impressed with Father for being able to do this.

But the example I was setting them worried my mother-in-law very much. She kept saying, "Suppose the children do this at the St. Francis Hotel!" I said, "Well, they're not likely to do that in the St. Francis Hotel." This idea that one always has to be setting an example or laying down a rule is a very burdensome way of looking at communication with children.

Against all this, the psychologist Carl Rogers, founder of "client-centered therapy," explored how far it is possible to go in helping children toward self-understanding and maturation if they are not given directives. The powers of self-direction and self-discipline inherent in the child were systematically explored by Rogers, Dorothy Baruch, and others—after being long overlooked because of activist preconceptions. With the discovery of such powers in children came a careful study of how these powers of self-direction could best be nurtured.

Many of our problems with our children are created by our unrealistic expectations of them. Supposing little Howard wets his pants. Is it a problem or isn't it? Well, this depends on two things. It depends first on how old Howard is, and second, it depends on *what we expect of a child of that age,* whatever that age may be. Is the fact that Susan eats messily at the table a problem? Again, it is or is not, depending on what our expectations are of a child of Susan's age. If we expect more of Howard or Susan than we have any right to expect at their developmental stage, we've really got a problem—that we created!

The advantage of living in our times is that we have, on the whole, better information than any previous generation on how children develop. Today the parents of a firstborn child can start out with the wisdom and relaxation and ability to predict that they formerly would have had to have five children to acquire.

Of course, what we believe about children today may not be the last word; there will be changes and corrections. But the extensionality of the approach, I think, is likely to last, because we live in an age in which there is some respect for the scientific gathering of data, especially about such matters as child development. And likely to last, too, I believe, is the realization that the child has certain needs and drives and a certain general pattern of development born in him. It is the job of parents to understand these patterns and go along with them, and to create an atmosphere in which the human personality can unfold. Now along with all this information comes the realization that human development is an extremely complex process—and I should emphasize both the complexity and the fact that it is a process. All sorts of forces are interrelated and never stand still. My wife wrote a few years ago, "If our son, Alan, gets into a fight at school, it affects his behavior at lunchtime. If the oldest girl in a family is feeling displaced by a younger sister, she may cling to her mother, sock her sister, pour the bathwater on the floor—all three or a dozen more behaviors may result. We can no longer view each item of behavior in a separate, compartmentalized pigeonhole. And when parents do view items of behavior in this way, they are likely to deal with them separately and therefore inadequately. For example, suppose you react to misbehavior at lunch by tightening up on the rules about table manners. You may be doing exactly the wrong thing, because the misbehavior at lunch may result from an emotional upset on the playground which has nothing to do with the lunch table, except that the human being is an interconnected creature so that all these events do have their connections within themselves."

What is the bearing of general semantics on these matters? First of all, training in general semantics gives a kind of readiness to receive and absorb and utilize the kind of information about children that scientific research has given us, because so much of what has been outlined here fits in perfectly with the principles of general semantics. There are, I am told, pediatricians who won't let mothers read baby books. The reason they forbid mothers to read is not that the books are bad, although some of them may be; it is that many mothers, unused to scientific ways of thinking, and perhaps overanxious too, often misread such books. Unaccustomed to distinguishing between levels of abstraction, they often confuse the general with the particular. To give an example, a woman wrote once in a letter to me: "If our baby wanted only two ounces of milk when the book said she should have eight, we used to waste an enormous amount of time and energy and emotion trying to coax her into taking what she didn't want." And the point about her comment is that until the difference between the *statistical* baby who wants eight ounces per feeding *on the average* and her *particular* baby who sometimes wanted two ounces and sometimes wanted twelve was pointed out to her, she was confusing the two and trying to give the baby eight ounces at each and every feeding. Now, if a statement about the number of ounces of milk an average baby needs can be so badly misread, think of the potential number of misunderstandings from more complicated statements in books such as those by Dorothy Baruch, Arnold Gesell, Margaret Ribble, and other child-rearing experts; think of all the statements there that can be misread if the mother is determined to misread them. But surely the solution to this problem of misreading need not be so drastic as to forbid mothers' reading.

Not only mothers but writers in newspaper columns and women's magazines seem also to be affected by this problem of misreading. When an authoritative writer opposes rigidity in methods of guiding children and urges permissiveness or nondirective methods, some popular interpreters, like some mothers, immediately make of permissiveness a dogmatic slogan. Then, a year or two later in the same popular journals there is a "reaction against permissiveness," with cries "that parents have rights too," and calls to "put father back at the head of the family." Thus there develops a shunting of opinion back and forth between the extremes (both absurd) of permissiveness and authoritarianism. Magazines and newspapers argue back and forth on these matters in cycles of about ten years. This kind of hassle is surely one that general semantics can teach us to avoid. We should be able to avoid making polarized, opposing dogmas out of otherwise useful generalizations.

Permissiveness is a tremendous idea. Permissiveness does not mean, and no one has ever meant it to mean, allowing children to break up the furniture or to pour hot soup on their little sister. Permissiveness means permitting children to do what they want, up to the point of not creating misery for others, not hurting others. But a more important component of permissiveness is that children should feel free to *express* their deepest feelings. Whether they do anything about them or not, they should always feel free to express them. Virginia Axline's *Play Therapy* describes a child, for example, who is very jealous of a little brother and pounds to pieces a doll representing little brother. This is a way of fully expressing feelings in order to understand them and master them. Therefore permissiveness means, among other things, symbolic or expressive permissiveness. Even in a therapy situation, however, actions are held within certain well-defined limits. But most people don't distinguish between words and actions very clearly. So even after having had permissiveness described to them in this way, people still sometimes say, "But you can't let the kids break up the furniture!"

Now, as to the matter of the dynamic complexity of a child's development, the general semantics orientation should prepare one for the fact that the whole is more than, and different from, the sum of the parts, and that one doesn't put in good advice here and get out good behavior there as if the child were a chewing-gum machine. Indeed, one of the first discoveries in general semantics is that communication is a complex matter indeed, about which too many people are hopelessly thoughtless and naive. The common assumption in communication is that you tell 'em, then you tell 'em again, and if they don't mind, hit 'em. For an enormous number of people this exhausts the repertory of their communicative techniques. In a Chicago newspaper there was a story of a child who fell out a third-story window and was killed. The mother, who was out of the house at the moment, was incredulous as well as grief-stricken. "I always spanked him for going near the open window," she said. As a matter of fact she had just spanked him for the same offense and had felt so bad about it that she had gone out to the corner to get him some ice cream when the tragedy happened—and she just couldn't understand it!

Words and Children

Those who still believe, after all the writing that semanticists have done, that semantics is a science of words, may be surprised to learn that semantics has the effect—at least, it has had on me and on many others—of reducing rather than increasing one's preoccupation with words. First of all, there is that vast area of nonverbal communication with children that we accomplish through holding, touching, rocking, caressing our children, putting food in their mouths, and all of the little attentions that we give them. These are all communication, and we communicate in this way for a long time before the children even start to talk.

Then, after they start to talk, there is always the problem of interpretation. There is a sense in which small children are recent immigrants in our midst. They have trouble both in understanding and in using the language, and they often make errors. Many people (you can notice this in the supermarkets, especially with parents of two- and three-year-old children) get angry at their children when they don't seem to mind. Anyone standing within earshot of one of these episodes can tell that the child just hasn't understood what the mother said. But the mother feels, "Well, I said it, didn't I? What's wrong with the child that he doesn't understand? It's English, isn't it?" But, as I say, the child is a recent immigrant in our midst and there are things that the child doesn't understand.

There are curious instances. Once, when our daughter was three years old, she found the bath too hot and she said, "Make it warmer." It took me a moment to figure out that she meant, "Bring the water more nearly to the condition we call warm." It makes perfectly good sense looked at that way. Confronted with unusual formulations such as these which children constantly make, many of us react with incredible lack of imagination. Sometimes children are laughed at for making "silly statements," when it only requires understanding their way of abstracting and their way of formulating their abstractions to see that they are not silly at all.

Children are newcomers to the language. Learning a language isn't just learning words; rules of the language are learned at the same time. Prove this? Very simple. Little children use a past tense like "I runned all the way to the park and I swimmed in the pool." "Runned" and "swimmed" are words they did not hear. They made them up by analogy from other past tenses they had heard. This means that they learned not only the vocabulary, they learned the rule for making the past tense—except that the English language doesn't follow its own rules. And when the child proves himself to be more logical than the English language, we take it out on the child—which is nonsense. Children's language should be listened to with great attentiveness and respect.

Again, when our daughter was three years old, I was pounding away at my typewriter in my study and she was drawing pictures on the floor when she suddenly said, "I want to go see the popentole."

I kept typing.

Then I stopped and said, "What?!"

She said, "I want to see the popentole."

"Did you say *popentole?*"

I just stopped. It was a puzzle to figure out, but I did. In a few seconds I said, "You mean like last Saturday, you want to go to Lincoln Park and see the totem pole?"

She said, "Yes."

And what was so warm about this, so wonderful about it, was that having got her point across, she played for another twenty minutes singing to herself, happy that she had communicated. I didn't say to her, "Okay, I'll take you next Sunday to see the popentole." The mere fact that she'd made her point and got it registered was a source of satisfaction to her. And I felt very proud of myself at the time for having understood.

One of the things we tend to overlook in our culture is the tremendous value of the acknowledgment of message. Not, "I agree with you" or "I disagree with you" or "That's a wonderful idea" or "That's a silly idea," but just the acknowledgment, "I know exactly what you've said. It goes on the record. You said that." She said, "I want to go see the totem pole." I said, "Okay, you want to go see the totem pole." The acknowledgment of message says in effect, "I know you're around. I know what you're thinking. I acknowledge your presence."

There is also a sense in which a child understands far more than we suspect. Because a child doesn't understand words too well (and also because his nervous system is not yet deadened by years spent as a lawyer, accountant, advertising executive, or professor of philosophy), a child attends not only to what we say but to everything about us as we say it—tone of voice, gesture, facial expression, bodily tensions, and so on. A child attends to a conversation between grown-ups with the same amazing absorption. Indeed, a child listening is, I hope, like a good psychiatrist listening—or like a good semanticist listening—because she watches not only the words but also the non-verbal events to which words bear, in all too many cases, so uncertain a relationship. Therefore a child is in some matters quite difficult to fool, especially on the subject of one's true attitude toward her. For this reason many parents, without knowing it, are to a greater or lesser degree in the situation of the worried mother who said to the psychiatrist to whom she brought her child, "I tell her a dozen times a day that I love her, but the brat still hates me. Why, doctor?"

"Life in a big city is dangerous," a mother once said to me. "You hear so often of children running thoughtlessly out in the street and being struck by passing cars. They will never learn unless you keep telling them and telling them." This is the communication theory that makes otherwise pleasant men and women into nagging parents: You've got to keep telling them; then you've got to remind them; then tell 'em again. Are there no better ways to teach children not to run out into the street? Of course there are. I think it was done in our family without words.

Whenever my wife crossed the street with our boy Alan—he was then about three—she would come to a stop at the curb whether there was any traffic in sight or not, and look up and down the boulevard before crossing. It soon became a habit.

One day I absentmindedly started crossing the street without looking up and down—the street was empty. Alan grabbed my coat and pulled me back on the curb to look up and down before we started out again. Children love to know the right way to do things. They learn by imitation far more than by precept.

The uncritical confidence that many people place in words is a matter of constant amazement to me. When we were living in Chicago there was a concrete courtyard behind our apartment house. I heard a great deal of noise and shouting out there one day, and I looked out and saw a father teaching his boy to ride a bicycle. The father was shouting instructions: "Keep your head up. Now push down with your left foot. Now look out, you're running into the wall. Steer away from it. *Steer away from it!* Now push down with your right foot. Don't fall down!" and so on and so on. The poor boy was trying to keep his balance, manage the bicycle, obey his father's instructions all at the same time, and he looked about as totally confused as it is possible for a little boy to get. One thing we learn from general semantics, if we haven't learned it some other way already, is that there are limits to what can be accomplished in words. Learning to ride a bicycle is beyond those limits. Having sensed those limits, we become content to let many things take care of themselves without words. All this makes for a quieter household.

The anthropologist Ray Birdwhistell has undertaken a study that he calls "kinesics,"* which is the systematic examination of gesture and body motion in communication; this is a rich area of concern about which many students of human behavior have been much excited. But there is a danger in going too far in this direction—in going overboard to the extent of saying that words are of *no* importance. There are thousands of things children must know and enjoy that it is not possible for them to get *without* words.

The sense of what one misses through the lack of words has been brought home to us by the fact that our second boy, Mark, now twenty-nine, is seriously mentally retarded. At the age of six he was hardly able to talk at all. Now he talks quite a bit, but his speech is very difficult to understand; members of the

* Ray Birdwhistell, *Kinesics and Context.* Philadelphia: University of Pennsylvania Press, 1970.

family can understand it about half the time. He was always able to understand words with direct physical referents—watch, glass of water, orange juice, record-player, television, and so on. But there are certain things that exist only in words, like the concept of the future. I remember the following incident when he was six years old. He came across a candy bar at ten minutes to twelve when lunch was just about to be served. I tried to take it away from him and said, "Look, Mark, you can have it right after lunch. Don't eat it now. You can have it right after lunch." Well, when he was six all he could understand was that it was being taken away from him *now,* and the idea that there was a future in which he'd have it back was something he just couldn't get at the time. Of course, the concept of futurity developed later, but it took him much longer to develop it than it took the other children.

For human beings, the future, which exists *only in language,* is a wonderful dimension in which to live. That is, human beings can readily endure and even enjoy postponement; the anticipation of future pleasures is itself a pleasure. But futurity is something that has no physical referent like "a glass of water." It exists only in language. Mark's frequent frustrations and rage when he was younger were a constant reminder to us that all the warmth and richness of nonverbal communication, all that we could communicate by holding him and feeding him and patting his head and playing on the floor with him, were not enough for the purposes of human interaction. Organized games of any kind all have linguistically formulated rules. Take an organized game like baseball. Can there be baseball without language? No, there can't. What's the difference between a ball and a strike? There are linguistically formulated rules by which we define the difference. All systematic games, even much simpler games that children play, have to have a language to formulate the rules. An enormous amount of human life is possible only with language, and without it one is very much impoverished.

Labeling

In psychological literature there is a lot about how it is necessary to have respect for each individual child, and educational literature is full of all sorts of theories about how the uniqueness of each child must be understood and attended to. Respect for the child is paid lip service in all democratic societies—that is, the respect for every human individual, including children. Like all generalizations, "respect for the individual," "respect for every child" are easy to say and they sound good at teachers' institutes. But they represent difficulties in practice because everybody believes that he already respects the child—in the same way that everybody believes in justice and also believes that his own actions are just. If we fail, then, to show sufficient respect for the uniqueness of the child, that failure is almost always unconscious. We do not, and indeed we cannot, know in what ways we are failing, because at the level of awareness we all think that we are doing fine.

Here is where general semantics can help us a great deal. General semantics trains us to expect and *look for* the unique differences in every individual, object, event, or person, so that we are ready not only to accept and understand the uniqueness of each child—not to expect this child to be like any other—but, on the other hand, not to have a faint dislike for other people's children because they're not like our own. There's no need to dwell on this, but notice what we do. We say to the child, "Why can't you stick to your piano practice? Shirley practices two hours a day." But this child is not Shirley. "It's high time Wilbur began to realize . . ." But Wilbur is a particular individual, not a statistical generalization. When a child is constantly being placed in judgment against a statistical generalization or against other children, in a very important sense the uniqueness of that child is *not* being respected.

A more subtle reason for the failure to respect a child is what I call a map-territory confusion. We each have a certain conception of our child inside our head. That's the map, the conceptual map of the child. Out there is the child himself, the territory. Now if we are given to map-territory confusion, we confuse our conception of the child with the child himself and therefore have unrealistic expectations or unfounded anxieties about him. Respect for the child, then, means keeping not only in touch but open-mindedly in touch with him, so that we can keep our conceptions changing from day to day and month to month as the child changes.

The semanticist Wendell Johnson, whose specialty was the study of stuttering, started out as a stutterer himself. In studying child development he discovered that *all* children, when they begin to talk, repeat words and syllables the way a stutterer does. Sometimes they repeat sounds eight or ten times before they get the word out. A child comes into the house—a little child about two and a half years old—in great excitement, and says, "Mommy, I saw, I saw, I saw . . ." He is far too excited to be able to say it calmly.

The mother's evaluation of this kind of utterance is of crucial importance. If she regards this repetitiousness as normal, she'll just wait for the child to finish the sentence. And that's all there is to it. But if she expects the speech fluency of an older child in a child who is only two and a half, then she may say, whether to herself or to the child, "What's wrong with the child? He's stuttering." Once she begins to *say* this, and *to react to what she has said,* she can make the child so self-conscious about his speech that he *becomes* a stutterer.

This is Wendell Johnson's semantogenic theory of stuttering—that stutterers are not born, they're made* by overconscientious and overanxious mothers. This theory may very well be true, because very often stutterers are first children, not the second, third, or fourth—certainly never the fifth, because mothers don't care by that time.

It is difficult to keep open-mindedly in touch with children

* Wendell Johnson, *People in Quandaries: The Semantics of Personal Adjustment.* New York: Harper & Brothers, 1946.

because we sabotage ourselves in this task by our own language habits. Somewhere along the line we verbalize our perceptions in conceptions. We say, "John is the musical one," "Eddy is so high-strung." Then we are likely to react no longer to John and Eddy as they actually are, but to what we have *said* about them. Furthermore some parents say such things, including extremely uncomplimentary statements, in the presence of the children themselves, thereby helping to fix, for better or worse—and often for worse—the child's own self-conception. The individual trained in general semantics is careful about this kind of labeling behavior. It is legitimate for parents, between themselves, to ask such questions and to discuss the child when he is not around—"I'm afraid Frank hasn't any artistic talent"—but not in front of Frank.

It is obvious that one should be as careful about labeling other people as about labeling the children. Parents say to their children, "Don't play with the Jones children. They're not our kind of people," or make remarks like, "God God, Jews are moving into that apartment upstairs." People say the most dreadful things. Then they wonder why their children have prejudices.

It's not necessary to be a student of general semantics to have arrived at such conclusions. General semantics is essentially a description of sane evaluation. If people are reasonably sane most of the time, general semantics is a description of how they already function, whether they have heard of general semantics or not. But some of us find it helps to have the general semantics scheme of things in mind. Take, for example, the concept of *evaluation*: the idea that events as we know them take place in the nervous systems of human beings; that no event is an objective fact independent of an evaluator—that is, no trip to the zoo, no Christmas present, no good-night hug, no cross word, no family meal, no book read aloud, exists for the participants without an evaluation being involved as its most important ingredient. In every situation between parent and child, and between children, evaluations are involved and these interact upon each other.

Think of the evaluations with which we browbeat children: "Eat your carrots, they're good for you." "Eat your custard, it's delicious." "That sand is wet, ugh." "That old wheel is dirty, put it down." "Don't touch those ashtrays, they're dirty." "You should *love* your little brother!" "Come here and say thank you. Your Aunt Bessie won't bring you any more presents unless you say thank you." "He's getting too fresh; got to show him where to head in." "That's just attention-getting behavior; ignore it." "Stop that crying, there's nothing to cry about." Now, these are mild examples; we needn't descend to the shocking levels of rudeness, strident commands, and physical violence that can be seen any day in a supermarket or on the playground. They represent the politer sins of forcing one's own evaluations on the child, or trying to—and one usually doesn't get away with it.

"This *is* good." "This *is* valuable." "This custard *is* delicious." "This is the way a way a big brother *should* feel." "That *is* attention-getting behavior." "There *is* no reason to cry." Is. Is. Is. The objective fact supported by the size and power of the parent. And no awareness that each of these phrases contains an evaluative factor. No saying, "This is how *I* evaluate it; does the child evaluate it that way?" Is a present desirable because it cost a lot of money? Because it appeals to the parent? What about the child's interest? Is the dirtiness the important thing about the old wheel or the ashtray? What about the child's right to explore the world? Isn't his freedom to explore, and feel, and find out about the world, important to him? Isn't it a very important question whether the custard is delicious *to him?* And politeness. How can one teach politeness, in this case saying "thank you," while at the very moment one is being impolite to the child, showing him up in front of Aunt Bessie? And what's wrong with attention-getting behavior? Isn't attention a legitimate demand? Do I want *my* attention-getting behavior ignored? God forbid! And what good is it to say, "There's nothing to cry about"? There obviously is or he wouldn't be crying.

A generalized consciousness of the fact that one always sees things in terms of his own evaluations, *and* that the child is doing the same, makes for a more flexible and more adaptable and much more effective approach to the problems that parents are constantly having to solve. This consciousness of evaluation need not be a matter of insecurity, or indefiniteness of opinion. When one is driving on a highway, just at the edge of consciousness is the white line that indicates the car is on the right side of the road. It isn't necessary to worry about that white line every second; it's there, it's at the edge of awareness. In the same way, certain rules of general semantics—like the knowledge of evaluative processes—act like that white line for the parent who makes use of them. He doesn't have to worry about them all the time. They're just there, and when he wanders away from them he begins to pull himself together and say, "What am I doing here?"

If we behave toward our children in general with this flexible attitude, with the attitude, "I'm not necessarily right, let's find out"; if we are aware of differences between one person and the next, one action and another action, one person at one time and the same person at another time; if we avoid crude, undifferentiated labeling and abstraction; if in answering our children's questions we are not perfunctory but try to answer them with all the extensionality at our command and within the child's grasp, then we shall substantially have answered the question, "How do you teach a child to be semantic?" We will have taught him by setting him an example.

We have a set of ceramic ashtrays at home, and when Alan was about six years old an aunt who was visiting said, "Pass me an ashtray." He said, "Which one?" There were six ashtrays in the set. My aunt said, "They're all the same, pass any one." Alan thereupon began to show my aunt in what ways each of these ashtrays was different from the other. My aunt no doubt thought he was being childish and silly, but I must say that we were at the moment very proud of him.

Father Knows Best—Sometimes

The famous Canadian psychiatrist Brock Chisholm aroused so much negative publicity in his speeches at the end of World War II that there were calls for his resignation as the first chairman of the World Health Organization of the United Nations. What he said that elicited the excited response was simply that, besides the economic and political causes of war, one of the contributory causes was the sense of guilt left in most people *as the result of their moral instruction*—or what most people call their moral instruction.

Suppose a father says to a child, "Don't do that! It gets on my nerves!" This is an invitation to an interesting experiment: Will Father get angry or won't he? So the child does it. It gets on Papa's nerves. Then Papa blows up and punishes him. What the father said is verified by the results of the experiment. "Stop doing that, you're going to make your little sister cry." The boy continues to do it. His little sister starts to cry. "If you continue playing with those dishes that way you're going to break one." So he continues playing with the dishes and drops one on the floor. It happened just as predicted.

Each of these instructions is, in a scientific sense, operational. If A, then B. If you do so-and-so, such-and-such will happen. If the child wants to do something enough he can take a chance on making his father angry; he can decide for himself whether to take the chance of making his sister cry or breaking one of the dishes. Having weighed the chances, he says, "I'll do it," or "I'll not do it." But notice that whenever you give an operational injunction of this kind, you ultimately leave it up to the child to decide what he wants to do.

But there is another, altogether different way of controlling the child, which is to say, "Don't do that. It's *wicked, naughty, bad, immoral.*" What do these words mean? Or, "Jesus will not love you if you do that!" How do you prove, after you've done it, that Jesus no longer loves you? There is no experimental method by which the prediction can be confirmed or disproved. "If you do that, you will never get to Heaven." The child is made to fear, but there is no way for him ever to find out if the consequences to his actions will follow as predicted. Let me quote my mother-in-law. Even at the age of eighty-three, she told this story with emotion. When she was three or four or five years old, her grandparents controlled her by saying, "Your dear, dead mother in Heaven is watching from the stars and knows everything you do." Even at her advanced age, it still upset her to recall the terror of that heavenly surveillance.

What a dirty trick! In principle, much that has traditionally been called morality has been controlling people by frightening them with nonoperational, nonverifiable statements. They were not encouraged to figure out what is proper behavior by the use of intelligence and social experience; they had to submit to control by threats of injury to their immortal soul and the fear of the flames of hell. What is produced by these methods is the opposite of morality—which I define as the power of self-control of the adequately socialized individual evaluating in the light of his own needs as well as the needs of others the desirability of bringing on known, predictable sequences of events through his own powers of choice.

Consider being brought up under this regime of "God will not love you if you do so-and-so." Most people brought up by these methods, says Brock Chisholm, are burdened for the rest of their lives by a sense of guilt—an unspecific sense of guilt that cannot, by the very nature of the means by which it was produced, ever be completely dispelled. Let me quote at some length from Dr. Chisholm's detailed account of how this is done. Commonly in childhood the process goes something like this:

1. Child does something he wants to.
2. Mother punishes or disapproves with accompanying "Bad, bad boy."
3. Child is afraid of physical punishment, or threatened loss of security in disapproval, and does not again commit same act when mother is there, but

4. Child does same thing when mother is not there.
5. Mother discovers child has done it again, sometimes "a little bird told me" or "God told me."
6. Mother punishes child.
7. Child stops doing it when mother is not there for the same reasons as (3) above, but he is now more confused with magic and more convinced of his essential badness.
8. Child imagines doing things he would like to do and often unguardedly indicates this to watchful parents.
9. Mother punishes or strongly disapproves of child's *thinking* things and frequently copes with the situation with "Remember God always knows what you are thinking."
10. Child has to control his thinking and make it "good," leaving no outlet whatever for all his normal and desirable urges and wishes, which by now are almost all labeled "bad." All the "original sin," the normally developing human urges, must be hidden even from himself by pretense, guilt, shame, and fear. . . .
11. During this same time other magics which prevent the development of clear thinking have been set up. Among these are fairies, Santa Claus, personification of animals and things, night skies in which stars are deceased relatives, babies brought by storks or in the doctor's bag or found under rose bushes, and many other distortions of reality. Unless he goes through a long and difficult process of reeducation it is probable that no child who has ever believed in any of these things can ever, throughout his life, think quite clearly and quite sanely about a wide variety of important things in his adult environment. This statement is not theory; it is quite provable.*

The result of this kind of miseducation is the crippling of man's most important gift—his power of imagination. Says Dr. Chisholm:

> Imagination provides a way of exploring without any real danger, of trespassing without being caught, of adventuring to gain experience without committing oneself in reality. Imagination is a scout that man may send in all directions— past, present, and future—to investigate all circumstances, activities, possibilities, and consequences.
> . . . If the scout (imagination) must be deaf to some things, blind to others, and may not feel still others, its value as a reliable source of information is greatly reduced.**

* G. Brock Chisholm, "Can Man Survive?" *ETC.*, 4, 1947, pp. 106–111.
** Ibid.

The crippling of intelligence by these bandages of belief, in the name of virtue and security for the soul, is as recognizable as the crippling of the feet of the Chinese girl who was sacrificed to the local concept of beauty. The result is, in both cases, not beauty of character or of feet, but distortion and crippling and loss of natural function. Intelligence, ability to observe and to reason clearly and to reach and implement decisions appropriate to the real situation in which he finds himself, are man's only specific methods of survival. His unique equipment is entirely in the anterior lobes of his brain. His destiny must lie in the direction indicated by his equipment. Whatever hampers or distorts man's clear true thinking works against man's manifest destiny and tends to destroy him.*

One of the occupational hazards of being a father (or a professor) is the temptation to play God. Being looked up to, he finds it necessary to know all the answers or to pretend that he does. Therefore, professors and parents all have some tendency to sound off before the young on topics about which they don't know very much. In one way or another they try to maintain the fiction that Father knows best. There has been a considerable revolt against this authoritarian figure of the father, and this revolt is manifest in almost every comic strip depicting domestic life. The father is ineffectual, helpless, silly, the legitimate butt of all jokes, the victim of all family strategy worked out by Mother and the children. Clarence Day's play *Life with Father* and Archie Bunker in the popular TV series *All in the Family* sum up brilliantly and cruelly both Father as authority figure and Father as damn fool. They are, of course, the same man.

One of the basic ideas of general semantics is that no one *can* know it all, no one *needs* to know it all, and that human beings can enjoy life, which is a never-ending quest, increasing knowledge and wisdom and predictability through experience, by keeping their minds open and flexible and hospitable to new information. General semantics also teaches that emotional security based on anything other than that openness of mind and ability to learn and adapt to new situations is illusory. What, then, is the role of the father in this new orientation? If, instead of being an authority figure, the answerer of all questions, he

* G. Brock Chisholm, "The Reestablishment of a Peacetime Society," *Psychiatry*, 9, 1946, pp. 3–20.

regards himself simply as a senior partner in a joint research enterprise, he will have found a solution. He answers his children's questions with: "This much I know, this I've heard, this I don't know. Let's investigate this together." If he does this, he is preparing his children, step by step, for the day when they will have to get along without him. Under such parental guidance it will not profoundly matter if Father himself is misinformed or wrong in many or most of his beliefs, because he will have given his children the curiosity to seek and find for themselves, and he will have already told them implicitly that there is no one place where they can expect to find all the answers. And he will also have given them the ability to revise their opinions with the passage of time and the acquisition of new information.

One of the terrible things about child psychologists of various schools is that they make the job of being a parent seem hopelessly complex. With vitamin deficiencies, Freudian theory, individual psychology theory, Jungian theory, conditioned reflex theory, and now general semantics theory to worry about, the problem of bringing up children seems just too much to contemplate without at least a Ph.D. But one doesn't need to worry too much. Much of the literature about children is written on the basis of the study of disturbed children; hence the emphasis has been upon the disorders of psychological development. Some people cannot read a medical book without feeling the symptoms of every disease described in the book. Similarly, when they read of the psychological disorders of children, of extremely sick children, some people cannot help projecting their own experiences and their own children into all the case histories. A parent who does this can make himself extremely miserable.

But there is also a lot of literature worth reading on the study of children in general—normal children, not sick children—and the implication in much of this literature is that children are amazingly hardy creatures. Hundreds of mistakes can be made in the handling of children and they survive. Instead of being damaged, they just grow smarter. Given a reasonable amount of care and affection, especially in their tenderest years, they grow, they mature, they develop insight—sometimes, it seems, in spite of the best efforts of their parents to gum things up.

Some of the finest young people I know were brought up

by parents whom I would judge to be hopelessly incompetent. In one case I remember when the children were tiny, I used to worry because their mother was so lazy. The mother was so shiftless that the children learned to take care of themselves extremely well; they grew up to be fine, remarkably self-reliant young people. Another set of parents were oversolicitous to the point of suffocating the child with attention and love, but the child managed to escape suffocation by finding enough associates outside the home, in friends' homes, to develop himself. In other words, there are many ways in which the child knows better than his parents do what he needs and what is good for him. So if parents provide the child with the basic security of love and attempted understanding, there are many matters about which they can relax.

All books, articles, and lectures about child care, including everything I am saying here, are at relatively high levels of abstraction—they are generalizations. But your child is not a generalization. He is a *particular* child, who has you for parents, your house for a home, a particular school to go to, a particular teacher, and a particular set of playmates on a particular street. What's right for him is not for any outsider to determine, not Gesell nor Spock nor Carl Rogers nor Brock Chisholm nor Lawrence Frank nor me nor anybody else. And often you will find yourself acting under the necessities of a particular situation without a single psychological theory or developmental chart to authorize you to do what you are doing. Under these conditions, if you can do what needs to be done firmly and without anxiety, because you know that no theory or body of theories can predict and cover every eventuality, you are well on the way to becoming an adequate parent—and maybe a semanticist, too.

Courtesy

Much of the literature of child psychology, including such books as Margaret Ribble's justly famous *The Rights of Infants*,* stresses the needs and rights of children—so that one is sometimes left with the impression that parents have no rights at all. However, as Thomas Gordon says in *Parent Effectiveness Training*,** parents do have needs and rights. They have their own lives to live, their own purposes to fulfill. Hence parents need effective ways to deal with children's behavior that interferes with parental needs.

Of course you can meet the problem head on, as most parents do, with such commands as "Stop wrinkling the paper," or "I'm going to get real angry if you don't get out from under my feet," or "Don't ever interrupt a person when he's reading," or "Why don't you go outside and play?" The first message commands him to do what he clearly does not want to do. The second threatens him. The third enunciates a general principle that you would not be willing to live by yourself. The fourth offers him a solution—your solution, not his.

Dr. Gordon is quite critical about this matter of "sending solutions." Parents may ask, "What's wrong with sending solutions? After all, isn't the child causing me the problem?" Yes, he is. However, a child, no less than an adult, resists being told what to do. Also, he may not like his parent's solution. Furthermore, the parent's sending a solution communicates another message: "I don't trust you to select a satisfactory solution by yourself." When the parent tells the child his solution, he is calling the shots. He is taking control. He is leaving the child out of it.

* New York: Columbia University Press, 1965.
** New York: Peter Wyden, 1970.

Essentially, there is a problem here of common courtesy—a courtesy everyone knows he owes to his friends and neighbors, and that he also owes to his own children.

If a friend was visiting your home and happened to put his feet on the rungs of a treasured antique chair, you surely would not say, "Get your feet off that chair this minute!" or "You should never put your feet on somebody's antique chair." No, friends are treated with more respect. You might say, "I'm embarrassed to mention this, but I just got that chair. It's an American eighteenth-century antique and I'm terribly afraid of getting it scratched." A message like this does not send a solution. It is not a "you-message." It is an "I-message." You-messages take the form, "You stop . . ." or "Don't you ever . . ." or "You should know better than . . ." or "Why don't you . . ." The you-message, stating or implying a direct criticism of the person addressed, is in its very nature discourteous.

However, when the parent simply tells the child how the child's behavior is affecting him, the message becomes an I-message: "I cannot rest when someone is crawling on my lap," or "I'm tired and I really don't feel like playing." "I want to rest" communicates what the parent is feeling. The you-message does not send the essential message, which is about the parent's needs—which are the central problem at the moment.

Actually, "You are being a pest" is a very poor way of communicating the parent's feelings of fatigue. "You are a pest" is a statement that cannot be understood by the child as anything but a negative evaluation of him. Telling someone how you feel—especially when the feelings are negative—is much less threatening than accusing him of causing those negative feelings. It is not likely to provoke a child's resistance and rebellion. Parents must be careful, however, that they are not sending disguised you-messages:

Father: "I feel strongly that you have been neglecting your chores."

Son: "How's that?"

Father: "Well, take your job of mowing the lawn. I feel upset every time you goof off, like last Saturday. I was angry at you because you sneaked off without mowing the backyard. I felt that that was irresponsible of you."

In this conversation the father has expressed his evaluations that his son was neglectful, a goof-off, sneaky and irresponsible. The statement "I feel you are a slob" is just as much a you-statement as "You are a slob." Parents must state exactly what they feel without adding their evaluations of the child: "I was disappointed," or "I wanted the lawn to look nice Sunday," or "I was upset because I thought we had agreed that the lawn would be mowed Saturday."

It is a curious convention that says that courtesy is something owed to friends and neighbors but not to children. Perhaps they need it more than anybody.

Our Son Mark

It was a terrible blow for us to discover that we had brought a retarded child into the world. My wife and I had had no previous acquaintance with the problems of retardation—not even with the words to discuss it. Only such words as imbecile, idiot, and moron came to mind. And the prevailing opinion was that such a child must be "put away," to live out his life in an institution.

Mark was born with Down's syndrome, popularly known as mongolism. The prognosis for his ever reaching anything approaching normality was hopeless. Medical authorities advised us that he would show some mental development, but the progress would be painfully slow and he would never reach an adolescent's mental age. We could do nothing about it, they said. They sympathetically but firmly advised us to find a private institution that would take him. To get him into a public institution, they said, would require a waiting period of five years. To keep him at home for this length of time, they warned, would have a disastrous effect on our family.

That was twenty-seven years ago. In that time, Mark has never been "put away." He has lived at home. The only institution he sees regularly is the workshop he attends, a special workshop for retarded adults. He is as much a part of the family as his mother, his older brother, his younger sister, his father, or our longtime housekeeper and friend, Daisy Rosebourgh.

Mark has contributed to our stability and serenity. His retardation has brought us grief, but we did not go on dwelling on what might have been, and we have been rewarded by finding much good in things the way they are. From the beginning, we have enjoyed Mark for his delightful self. He has never seemed like a burden. He was an "easy" baby, quiet, friendly, and passive; but he needed a baby's care for a long time. It was easy to be patient with him, although I must say that some of his stages, such as his love for making chaos, as we called it, by pulling all the books he could reach off the shelves, lasted much longer than normal children's.

Mark seems more capable of accepting things as they are than his immediate relatives; his mental limitation has given him a capacity for contentment, a focus on the present moment, which is often enviable. His world may be circumscribed, but it is a happy and bright one. His enjoyment of simple experiences— swimming, food, birthday candles, sports-car rides, and cuddly cats—has that directness and intensity so many philosophers recommend to all of us.

Mark's contentment has been a happy contribution to our family, and the challenge of communicating with him, of doing things we can all enjoy, has drawn the family together. And seeing Mark's communicative processes develop in slow motion has taught me much about the process in all children.

Fortunately Mark was born at a time when a whole generation of parents of retarded children had begun to question the accepted dogmas about retardation. Whatever they were told by their physicians about their children, parents began to ask: "Is that so? Let's see." For what is meant by "retarded child"? There are different kinds of retardation. Retarded child No. 1 is not retarded child No. 2, or 3, or 4. Down's syndrome is one condition, while brain damage is something else. There are different degrees of retardation, just as there are different kinds of brain damage. No two retarded children are exactly alike in all respects. Institutional care *does* turn out to be the best answer for some kinds of retarded children or some family situations. The point is that one observes and reacts to the *specific* case and circumstances rather than to the generalization.

This sort of attitude has helped public understanding of the nature and problems of retardation to become much deeper and more widespread. It's hard to believe now that it was "definitely known" twenty years ago that institutionalization was the "only way." We were told that a retarded child could not be kept at home because "it would not be fair to the other children." The family would not be able to stand the stress. "Everybody"

believed these things and repeated them, to comfort and guide
the parents of the retarded.

We did not, of course, lightly disregard the well-meant advice
of university neurologists and their social-worker teams, for they
had had much experience and we were new at this shattering
experience. But our general semantics, or our parental feelings,
made us aware that their reaction to Mark was to a generalization,
while to us he was an individual. They might have a valid generalization about statistical stresses on statistical families, but they
knew virtually nothing about our particular family and its evaluative processes.

Mark was eight months old before we were told he was retarded. Of course we had known that he was slower than the
average child in smiling, in sitting up, in responding to others
around him. Having had one child who was extraordinarily ahead
of such schedules, we simply thought that Mark was at the other
end of the average range.

In the course of his baby checkups, at home and while travel-
ing, we had seen three different pediatricians. None of them
gave us the slightest indication that all was not well. Perhaps
they were made uncertain by the fact that Mark, with his part
Japanese parentage, had a right to have "mongolian" features.
Or perhaps this news is as hard for a pediatrician to tell as it
is for parents to hear, and they kept putting off the job of telling
us. Finally, Mark's doctor did suggest a neurologist, indicating
what his fears were, and made an appointment.

It was Marge who bore the brunt of the first diagnosis and
accompanying advice, given at the university hospital at a time
when I had to be out of town. Stunned and crushed, she was
told: "Your husband is a professional man. You can't keep a
child like this at home."

"But he lives on love," she protested.

"Don't your other children live on love, too?" the social worker
asked.

Grief-stricken as she was, my wife was still able to recognize
a non sequitur. One does not lessen the love for one's children
by dividing it among several.

"What can I read to find out more about his condition and
how to take care of him?" Marge asked.

"You can't get help from a book," answered the social worker. "You must put him away."

Today this sounds like dialogue from the Dark Ages. And it *was* the Dark Ages. Today professional advice runs generally in the opposite direction: "Keep your retarded child at home if it's at all possible."

It was parents who led the way: They organized into parents' groups; they pointed out the need for preschools, schools, diagnostic centers, work-training centers, and sheltered workshops to serve the children who were being cared for at home; they worked to get these services, which are now being provided in increasing numbers. But the needs are a long way from being fully met.

Yet even now the cost in money—not to mention the cost in human terms—is much less if the child is kept at home than if he is sent to the institutions in which children are put away. And many of the retarded are living useful and independent lives, which would never have been thought possible for them.

But for us at that time, as for other parents who were unknowingly pioneering new ways for the retarded, it was a matter of going along from day to day, learning, observing, and saying, "Let's see."

There was one more frightening hurdle for our family to get over. On that traumatic day Marge got the diagnosis, the doctor told her that it was too risky for us to have any more children, that there was a fifty percent chance of our having another mongoloid child. In those days, nothing was known of the cause of mongolism. There were many theories. Now, at least, it is known to be caused by the presence of an extra chromosome, a fault of cell division. But the question "Why does it happen?" had not yet been answered.

Today, genetic counseling is available to guide parents as to the probabilities of recurrence on a scientific basis. We were flying blind. With the help of a doctor friend, we plunged into medical books and discovered that the doctor who gave us the advice was flying just as blind as we were. No evidence could be found for the fifty percent odds. Although there did seem to be some danger of recurrence, we estimated that the probabilities were with us. We took the risk and won.

Our daughter, Wynne, is now twenty-five. She started as

Mark's baby sister, soon passed him in every way, and really helped bring him up. The fact that she had a retarded brother must have contributed at least something to the fact that she is at once delightfully playful and mature, observant, and understanding. She has a fine relationship with her two brothers.

Both Wynne and Alan, Mark's older brother, have participated, with patience and delight, in Mark's development. They have shown remarkable ingenuity in instructing and amusing him. On one occasion, when Mark was not drinking his milk, Alan called him to his place at the table and said, "I'm a service station. What kind of car are you?" Mark, quickly entering into the make-believe, said, "Pord."

Alan: "Shall I fill her up?"

Mark: "Yes."

Alan: "Ethyl or regular?"

Mark: "Reg'lar."

Alan (bringing the glass to Mark's mouth): "Here you are."

When Mark finished his glass of milk, Alan asked him, "Do you want your windshield cleaned?" Then, taking a napkin, he rubbed it briskly across Mark's face, while Mark grinned with delight. This routine became a regular game for many weeks.

Alan and Wynne interpret and explain Mark to their friends, but never once have I heard them apologize for him or deprecate him. It is almost as if they judge the quality of other people by how they react to Mark. They think he is "great," and expect their friends to think so too.

Their affection and understanding were shown when Wynne flew to Oregon with Mark to visit Alan and his wife, Cynthea, who went to college there. Wynne described the whole reunion as "tremendous" and especially enjoyed Mark's delight in the trip.

"He was great on the plane," she recalls. "He didn't cause any trouble except that he rang the bell for the stewardess a couple of times when he didn't need anything. He was so great that I was going to send him back on the plane alone. He would have enjoyed that." But she didn't, finally, because she didn't trust others to be able to understand his speech or to know how to treat him without her there to give them clues.

Mark looks reasonably normal. He is small for his age (about five feet tall) and childlike. Anyone who is aware of these matters would recognize in him some of the characteristic symptomatic features, but they are not extreme. His almost incomprehensible speech, which few besides his family and teachers can understand, is his most obvious sign of retardation.

Mark fortunately does not notice any stares of curiosity he may attract. To imagine how one looks in the eyes of others takes a level of awareness that appears to be beyond him. Hence he is extremely direct and totally without self-consciousness.

I have seen him come into our living room, walk up to a woman he has never seen before, and kiss her in response to a genuinely friendly greeting. Since few of us are accustomed to such directness of expression—especially the expression of affection—the people to whom this has happened are deeply moved.

Like other children, Mark responds to the evaluations of others. In our family, he is accepted just as he is. Because others have always treated him as an individual, a valued individual, he feels good about himself, and, consequently, he is good to live with. In every situation between parent and child or between children, evaluations are involved—and these interact on each other. Certainly, having Mark at home has helped us be more aware and be more flexible in our evaluations.

This kind of sensitivity must have carried over into relations between the two normal children, because I cannot remember a single real fight or a really nasty incident between Alan and Wynne. It's as if their readiness to try to understand Mark extended into a general method of dealing with people. And I think Marge and I found the same thing happening to us, so that we became more understanding with Alan and Wynne than we might otherwise have been. If we had time and patience for Mark, why not for the children who were quick and able? We knew we could do serious damage to Mark by expecting too much of him and being disappointed. But how easy it is to expect too much of bright children and how quickly they feel your disappointment! Seeing Mark's slow, slow progress certainly gave us real appreciation of the marvelous perception and quick learning processes of the other two, so that all we had to do was open our eyes and our ears, and listen and enjoy them.

I don't want to sound as if we were never impatient or obtuse as parents. We were, of course. But parents need to be accepted as they are, too. And I think our children—bless their hearts—were reasonably able to do so.

With Mark, it was easy to feel surprise and delight at any of his accomplishments. He cannot read and will never be able to. But he can pick out on request almost any record from his huge collection—Fleetwood Mac, or the Rolling Stones, or Christmas carols—because he knows so well what each record looks like. Once we were discussing the forthcoming marriage of some friends of ours, and Mark disappeared into his playroom to bring out, a few minutes later, a record with the song "A House, a Car, and a Wedding Ring."

His love of music enables him to figure out how to operate almost any record changer or hi-fi set. He never tries to force a piece of machinery because he cannot figure out how it works, as brighter people often do. And in a strange hotel room, with a TV set of unknown make, it is Mark—not Marge or I—who figures out how to turn it on and get a clear picture. As Alan once remarked: "Mark may be retarded, but he's not stupid!"

Of course, it has not all been easy—but when has easiness been the test of the value of anything? To us, the difficult problems that must be faced in the future only emphasize the value of Mark as a person.

What does that future hold for Mark?

He will never be able to be independent; he will always have to live in a protected environment. His below-50 IQ reflects the fact that he cannot cope with unfamiliar situations.

Like most parents of the retarded, we are concentrating on providing financial security for Mark in the future, and fortunately we expect to be able to achieve this. Alan and his wife and Wynne have all offered to be guardians for Mark. It is wonderful to know they feel this way. But we hope that Mark can find a happy place in one of the new residence homes for the retarded.

The residence home is something new and promising and it fills an enormous need. It is somewhat like a club, or a family, with a housemother or manager. The residents share the work around the house, go out to work if they can, share in recreation and companionship. Away from their families, who may be over-protective and not aware of how much the retarded can do for themselves (are we not guilty of this, too!), they are able to live more fully as adults.

An indication that there is still much need for public education about the retarded here in California is that there has been difficulty in renting decent houses for this kind of home. Prospective neighbors have objected. In some ways the Dark Ages are still with us; there are still fear and hostility where the retarded are concerned.

Is Mark able to work? Perhaps. He thrives on routine and enjoys things others despise, like clearing the table and loading the dishwasher. To Mark, it's fun. It has been hard to develop in him the idea of work, which to so many of us is "doing what you don't want to do because you have to." We don't know yet if he could work in a restaurant loading a dishwasher. In school, he learned jobs like sorting and stacking scrap wood and operating a delightful machine that swoops the string around and ties up a bundle of wood to be sold in the supermarket. That's fun, too.

He is now in a sheltered workshop where he can get the kind— the one kind—of pleasure he doesn't have much chance for. That's the pleasure of contributing something productive and useful to the outside world. He does various kinds of assembling jobs, packaging, sorting, and simple machine operations. He enjoys getting a paycheck and cashing it at the bank. He cannot count, but he takes pride in reaching for the check in a restaurant and pulling out his wallet. And when we thank him for dinner, he glows with pleasure.

It's a strange thing to say, and I am a little startled to find myself saying it, but often I feel that I wouldn't have had Mark any different.

PART II
MAN AND WOMAN

Semantics and Sexuality

There are many puzzles about human sexuality. As one goes up the scale of biological complexity, the infant mortality rate goes steadily downward. In contrast to the millions that fish give birth to in order to ensure the continuance of their species, amphibians such as frogs reproduce in the thousands, reptiles in the hundreds, mammals and birds in the dozens.

The increasing complexity of organisms as they move up the evolutionary scale is accompanied by the increasing length of the dependency of the young. The striped bass is on his own in the hostile waters of the San Joaquin River from the moment he is a fertilized egg. For him there is no period of maturation within a shelled egg, or inside the warmth of a maternal womb, before being thrown on his own resources. But infants of higher forms of life are fed and nurtured in their nest in infancy. A puppy is well on his way to being a well-formed dog when he is born, but he is still suckled and cared for many months after birth. During infancy, all mammals experience a period of dependency during which they undergo some kind of education from their elders. The period of dependency has an enormously important function. The longer the period of infant dependency in any creature, the greater the reliance in later life on information gathering and processing as its survival mechanism and the less its reliance upon built-in reflexes, usually called instincts.

Biological complexity is essentially a matter of the ability of an organism to take in and utilize for purposes of survival more and more information about the environment. The octopus and the oyster, both of the phylum Mollusca, provide a fascinating contrast. Oysters, in the interests of survival, gave up locomotion; they attached themselves to rocks and covered themselves

39

with hard shells, which, along with their fantastic birthrate, are their basic survival mechanisms. Oysters sacrificed a lot in order to achieve security; they have few adventures. If you stay in one place all of your life, you don't get to know very much. That is the lesson of the oyster.

The octopus, in contrast, with no hard shell to protect him, was compelled to keep moving. He developed techniques of rapid locomotion, concealment, and food entrapment in order to survive. The octopus, as the British biologist J. Z. Young has shown, is by far the smartest of the Mollusca, capable of learning and even of certain elementary kinds of problem solving.* Mobility brings a creature in contact with many aspects of the environment and, therefore, inevitably develops intelligence.

Or take the matter of the warm-bloodedness of mammals. The cold-blooded animal is the prisoner of temperature. In cold weather, it slows down to a complete halt—like the alligators that lie motionless at the bottom of the pool in the Sacramento zoo in January. The warm-blooded animals, including the birds, maintain body heat despite outside temperatures. Able to stay cool in hot climates and to stay warm in cold climates, mammals have great mobility; they can live in far more places than reptiles.

Warm-bloodedness is inextricably connected with mobility, with expanded opportunities for information gathering and, therefore, intelligence. The dominant characteristics of the higher mammals consist of the anatomical and nervous structures necessary to take in and use a great abundance of information together with the habits of sociability to ensure the sharing of that information.

These characteristics achieve their highest development in man, whom Weston La Barre calls "the human animal," and Desmond Morris, the "naked ape."** It is of enormous human consequence that our remote ancestors lived in trees, where they were safe from prowling quadrupeds, such as tigers and jaguars. Anatomical adaptation made life in the trees possible. The grasping hands and feet and the ability to rotate the arms in their sockets permitted locomotion in the treetops; the eyes

---

* *Doubt and Certainty in Science: A Biologist's Reflections on the Brain.* New York: Oxford University Press, 1951.

** Weston La Barre, *The Human Animal.* Chicago: University of Chicago Press, 1954; Desmond Morris, *The Naked Ape.* New York: McGraw-Hill, 1967.

side by side at the front of the face, not at the sides of the head as in quadrupeds, provided binocular vision, essential to the accurate judging of distances when swinging from branch to branch. A horse cannot scratch its own back; monkeys and people can. With the hand at the end of a brachiating, jointed arm, monkeys and human beings grasp things, bring them close to inspect them with their binocular eyes, put things in their mouth to taste or bite. These are all primate ways of taking in detailed information about the world. A small baby who puts things in his mouth shouldn't be slapped: the baby is merely being true to his basic nature. It is simpler not to leave things around that are unsafe—but to make sure to leave a number of things around that the child may bite and taste and chew and spit out as part of his education.

Tree-dwelling creatures are always in danger of falling from their perches despite their grasping hands and feet. The species of tree-dwelling primates that developed the principle of having one baby at a time and taking extremely good care of it survived; thus ape and human mothers have one pair of teats high up on the chest, rather than a long row of them along the whole underside, like sows.

The baby of the tree-dwelling primate was born with an instinct, which human babies are also born with, for grasping with its hands the fur of its mother and sustaining its own weight. An extremely close interindividual process develops between baby and mother. Babies hold their mothers and are held; they are cuddled and rocked and played with and carried from place to place. The mammalian process of suckling gives gratification to both baby and mother, making them necessary to each other. Some larger quadrupeds—for example, the elephant—like the higher primates, have one baby at a time and also develop an intense mother-child relationship.

The cherishing of each individual life is not simply a moral demand peculiar to highly developed civilizations. It is a basic demand of uniparous mammals, including elephants, who attempt furiously to save each other's life and mourn deeply the death of one of their group.*

For the purposes of taking in information, human beings have

* Iain Oria and Douglas Hamilton, *Among the Elephants*. New York: The Viking Press, 1975.

great visual acuity, excellent hearing, an extraordinarily delicate sense of touch (especially at lips and tongue and fingertips), a nervous system that transmits data with great rapidity, but a very limited sense of smell—not one-tenth as acute as that of the dog and even less acute than that of the elephant, who holds up the wet tip of his proboscis and turns it from side to side like radar to detect faint odors from any direction.

Weston La Barre says that the sense of smell is subordinated in the tree-dwelling primates because of the greater importance of vision to creatures living high above the ground. But he further suggests that the sense of smell may well have been repressed. Baby primates clinging to their mothers would keep her fur soiled. Nests would frequently be fouled. Perhaps the repression of smell was necessary among higher primates so that they could endure each other at close quarters.

Whatever the evolutionary facts may be, Professor La Barre's suggestion certainly fits in with a common observation, that people usually prefer smelly company to no company at all—and as soon as they are absorbed in socializing they don't notice the smells anymore. Any crowded dance hall or nightclub gives evidence of the ease with which human beings adjust to strong odors—to say nothing of the smell of some large cities, even without a garbage men's strike.

But the most important fact about human beings is their non-seasonal sexuality. Almost all other creatures have a mating season, an estrous cycle, periods of being in heat interspersed with long periods of sexual quiescence or apathy. The female of many mammals is sexually receptive only during ovulation, which, as in the porcupine, according to Sally Carrighar in *Wild Heritage,** is only once a year.

Male sea lions attend their females during the mating season, but as soon as the mating is over, they take off, leaving the care of the young to the females. They go hunting—or go to the club to shoot pool, or whatever it is that menfolk do when they're by themselves—and they don't reappear until next mating season. But human beings are different. The adult male is capable of being sexually aroused with or without provocation at practically any time. Although female receptivity is interrupted

* Boston: Houghton Mifflin, 1965.

by childbirth, it is not by pregnancy, and shortly after birth is over, the female is back in business again. Human beings are just about always interested in sex. "Never on Sunday" may be a professional rule but it is not a biological one.

At first it seems quite illogical that human beings, with the great reproductive economy that enables them to continue the race and multiply while bearing only a few young, should be so permanently and obsessively interested in sex. Sexual activity in human beings, as Weston La Barre says, serves two purposes— not merely procreation, but recreation. With his nonseasonal sexual interest, the male does not leave the female to bring up the young by herself. Baby and mother are tied to each other by suckling and by the prolonged dependency of the human infant. The male is tied to the mother by sexual interest—and has to learn to get along with the children. The advantage to the species is that the young of an information-gathering class of life have much to learn from the father as well as the mother.

Thus the lifelong patterns of human communication and inter-action are learned in the family. Sons and daughters learn to relate to mothers and fathers and to each other. This basic train-ing in communication will serve them all their lives. And Freudi-ans are quite right in attributing many of the difficulties of adult life to unresolved problems of communication and interrelation-ship left over from childhood experience. As the child grows up it needs another relationship as stable and as strong as its relationship has been to the mother.

Because in mature pairing a deep and lasting friendship is sought, human courtship is more protracted, more elaborate, than that of any other creature. There is a vast amount of small talk in courtship—the exchange of words not for the sake of transmitting information so much as for the sake of assessing the interpersonal climate or evoking emotional states. If each hears in the voice of the other the affection and reassurance evocative of the sounds they heard as babies from their own parents, they feel more and more at ease with each other.

Courtship for human beings is an immense communicative process. Dancing together, picnicking, going to ball games or movies, talking and teasing and testing each other, the couple finds occasion after occasion for comparing each other's reac-tions to the world, adjusting to each other, trying to decide if there is enough depth to the relationship to make it a durable one.

All the senses are brought into play. Assessments of the partner's sincerity or insincerity, gentleness or callousness, thoughtfulness or selfishness are made by reading subverbal as well as verbal cues: the way one's partner holds one's hand, takes one's arm, returns one's gaze. The long courtship is certainly an essential part of what Morris calls sexual imprinting. As the songwriters say, it is the touch of *your* hand, it is *your* smile, *your* hair, that mean so much to me—and not someone else's hand or smile or hair.

And when it comes to mating, this too, like courtship, is richer for human beings than for other animals. "In baboons," says Morris, "the time taken from mounting to ejaculation is no more than seven to eight seconds . . . the female does not appear to experience any kind of climax." For human beings, sex is infinitely sexier than for the baboon: "the hunting life that gave us naked skins and more sensitive hands has given us much greater scope for sexually stimulating body-to-body contacts. . . . Stroking, rubbing, pressing and caressing occur in abundance and far exceed anything found in other primate species. Also, specialized organs such as lips, earlobes, nipples, breasts and genitals are richly endowed with nerve endings and have become highly sensitized to erotic tactile stimulation."* Just as important as the tactile signals are the visual signals—the responsive facial expression of the partner—and the auditory signals—the voice husky with sexual excitement.

Sexual union then is a profound person-to-person communication, the culmination of all the communications antecedent to it. The sexually attractive and the sexually sensitive areas of the body are largely in front. It is therefore by no means accidental that a vast majority of the human race unite sexually in face-to-face position. "The frontal approach means that the in-coming sexual signals and rewards are kept tightly linked with identity signals from the partner," writes Morris. "Face-to-face sex is 'personalized sex.' "

In other words we are so constructed as to derive additional sexual pleasure from knowing whom we're sleeping with. The

---

* Morris, p. 66.

sexual act derives richness from all the prior imprintings of the valued partner. And sexual pleasure is cumulative, each imprinting reinforcing the effect of past imprintings.

Sexual anarchists and advocates of sexual freedom proclaim that the general attitudes and legislation in favor of durable monogamous relationships are merely cultural prejudices, and that monogamy is contrary to human nature. Although Morris uses the term "pair-bond" in place of "monogamy" and "imprinting" in place of "love," he offers new grounds for questioning the easy dogmatism of sexual-freedom advocates about the nature of human nature.

For human beings, sexual imprintings necessarily involve communicative printings. Reinforcing the sensual pair-bond for a couple who have lived together for many years are all the communications they have exchanged, the understandings they have established, the feelings they have shared. They have talked to each other about themselves, their friends, the adventures they have had, their home, their financial problems, their children, their political decisions, and their philosophies. For the talkative class of life, a pair-bond is never solely the result of conditioning to mutually pleasurable erotic sensations. In the human pair-bond, the erotic is inextricably bound up with the semantic.

Nature has so distributed our nerve endings and constructed our bodies and brains that the profoundest joy we can experience comes from an erotic-semantic attachment reinforced by repeated imprintings over a long period of time. Like a work of art, a durable pair-bond is not instinctually given. It is an achievement, and like all other worthwhile human achievements, it is the product of patience, thought, and self-discipline. Good communication is therefore at the heart of good sexuality.

Sex Is Not a Spectator Sport

In current discussions of pornography and obscenity, there is widespread confusion about two matters. First there is sexual behavior and what it means to the participants. Secondly there is the outside observer of that sexual behavior and what it means to him. When a man and a woman make love, enjoying themselves and each other fully and unself-consciously, a rich relationship is reaffirmed and made richer by their lovemaking. However beautiful or sacred that love relationship may be to that man and woman, it would have an entirely different significance to a Peeping Tom, secretly watching the proceedings from outside the window. The sexual behavior is not itself obscene. Obscenity is peculiarly the evaluation of the outside observer. Theoretically the actors may themselves be made the observers. If, for example, unknown to the man and woman, a movie were to be made of their lovemaking, and that movie were to be shown to them later, that lovemaking might take on an entirely different significance. What was performed unself-consciously and spontaneously might be viewed later by the actors themselves with giggling or shame or shock. They might even insist that the film be destroyed—which is entirely different from saying that they would stop making love.

What I am saying is that obscenity and pornography can happen only when sexual events are seen from the outside, from a spectator's point of view. This is the crux of the pornography problem. Pornography is sexual behavior made public through symbolization—by representation in literature, by simulation or enactment in a nightclub act or on stage, by arts such as painting, photography, or the movies. To object to pornographic movies or art is not, as some would have us believe, a result of hang-ups about sex. One may be completely healthy and still object to many of the current representations of sexual acts in the movies and on the stage.

Standards of morality are one thing. Standards of decorum are another. There is nothing immoral about changing one's clothes or evacuating one's bowels. But in our culture people as a rule do not change their clothing in the presence of the other sex, excepting their spouses. Men and women have separate public lavatories, and within them each toilet is in a separate compartment for privacy. Love too needs privacy. Human beings normally make love in private, whether that love is socially sanctioned, as in marriage, or unsanctioned, as in a house of prostitution.

The trouble with sexual intercourse as an object of artistic or literary representation is that its meaning is not apparent in the behavior. Hence serious writers have historically been reticent in their descriptions of sex. In Dante's *Divine Comedy* Francesca tells of her tragic love for Paolo. They were reading an ancient romance, and as they read, their passions suddenly overcame them. What happened? Dante simply has Francesca say, "That day we read no further." The rest is left to the reader's imagination—and the reader cannot help feeling the power of that onrushing, fatal passion.

Men and women couple with each other for a wide variety of reasons. Sometimes the sexual encounter is the fulfillment of true love and respect for each other. Sometimes it is an expression of drunken irresponsibility. Sometimes one of the partners is using sex as an instrument of exploitation or aggression against the other. Sometimes sex is a commercial transaction, with either party being the prostitute. Sometimes sex is the expression of neurosis. Sometimes it is evidence of people getting over their neuroses. However, to the movie camera, as to a Peeping Tom, they are all "doing the same thing." To concentrate on the mechanics of sex is to ignore altogether its human significance.

Today movies do not stop at exhibiting copulation. Every kind of aberrant sexual behavior and sadomasochistic perversion is being shown. The advertisements in the newspaper before me announce such titles as *Nude Encounter, Too Hot to Handle, Deep Throat, The Devil in Miss Jones, The Passion Parlor, Hot Kitten,* and *Honeymoon Suite,* as well as "16 hours of hard-core male stag."

The only purpose of movies such as these, from all I can tell from advertisements and reviews, is, as D. H. Lawrence expressed it, "to do dirt on sex." Let the American Civil Liberties Union fight for the right of these movies to be shown. I will not.

Compatibility

The late Eric Berne's famous book *Games People Play** offers a novel analysis of person-to-person communication. He said that human beings have three "ego states," or states of mind, which he called Parent, Adult, and Child. The Parent in you is protective, admonitory, often scolding or censorious, as your own parents were to you when you were a child. The Adult in you is busy taking in information about the environment and solving problems in the light of that information. The Child is playful, imaginative, mischievous, irresponsible, exasperating, and lovable.

Dr. Berne's theory was most quickly illustrated by his own example. He bought an expensive car when his book became successful. He explained that his Child—that is, the Child in him—bought it; his Adult paid for it; his Parent told him not to drive too fast.

Now, in any love relationship, all people have their emotional ups and downs. Couples who get along supremely well are those profoundly attuned to each other's moods. Most of the time the man and woman relate to each other as Adults, discussing realistically their finances, their children's education, their social obligations, or whatever. Sometimes, however, the woman is ill or nervous or anxious or afraid and needs protection, in which case the man can be a Parent to her Child. She is "baby" who can depend on "Big Daddy" to protect her. But sometimes it's the other way. The man has had reverses in business or career. He is anxious or discouraged. At this point, the woman is Parent, the loving mother who protects and strengthens her little boy.

* New York: Grove Press, 1964.

Sometimes, as they worry about their children, and especially about their children's friends, they talk as Parent to Parent; and the favorite remark of communication at this level is, "What *is* the younger generation coming to?" Then when the man and woman make love, they may become teasing, giggly, playful, spontaneous, emotionally expressive—a Child-to-Child relationship.

A complete love relationship over a long period of time necessarily means, then, sensitivity to the moods of the other and the ability to respond to them. If the woman cannot be the big strong mother when her big strong husband is for the time being a frightened little boy, or if the man cannot be the protective father when his wife is a scared little girl, then there's something lacking in the relationship. Even more seriously, if either one remains persistently the Child when adult thinking and adult decisions are called for, there is something very much wrong in the relationship.

In courtship, one can easily be misled by a pleasant Child-to-Child relationship; the couple go to parties and dances and the girl can say, "But he's such *fun* to be with!" After marriage, however, it is sometimes discovered, too late, that the boy who was such fun to be with is incurably a boy, incapable of assuming adult responsibilities.

So to young people going steady but not yet married, perhaps it would be good advice to say: It's nice that you have such good times together. But don't marry until you've faced some kind of serious problem together—not interpersonal problems between yourselves, but problems given by the world around you. If you can gain strength from each other by confronting this problem, if your respect for each other increases as you discover each other's emotional and intellectual resources, maybe you *are* meant for each other.

Finding Out Who You Are

The concept of selfhood starts being built when the person is still a baby, lying in his crib, reaching out around him. The baby touches his toes and touches the sides of the crib and begins to define what is "me" and what is "not me." Then parents hover over him, pick him up and cuddle him, and he learns "I am loved" or "I am not loved." The way in which he is held is a form of communication that says, "You are the most precious thing in the world," or, "Good grief, why did you have to happen to me?"

Out of the confusion of things going on around the little baby, certain regular patterns of sound become recognizable. "Larry," "Larry, dear," "Are you awake, Larry?" "Are you hungry, Larry?" and soon he learns that he is Larry and not someone else—and another step has been taken in his self-definition.

Every baby has a potentiality of going in any direction. She (or he) can become a mechanic or a philosopher or a criminal. These potentialities exist in all of us, but the society around us, consciously or unconsciously, pushes us in one direction or another.

To begin with, a different self-concept is built into little boys from that which is built into little girls. The caretaker of the apartment house we lived in many years ago in Chicago was a man of many skills—a combination plumber, carpenter, electrician, mason, mechanic. And he was very proud of his skills. When his son turned four, the boy picked up a hammer and started trying to nail two pieces of wood together. His father was enormously pleased—indeed, quite excited. He went downtown that very afternoon to buy his son a little carpentry set to encourage him in this direction. About a year later, his daughter turned four. She began, like her older brother, to play with a hammer and a saw. The father simply laughed and said, "She thinks she is going to be a carpenter. Ha, ha!" and that was the end of that.

Parents tend to ignore that which is defined as "feminine behavior" in a boy and encourage "masculine behavior." They encourage what they define as "femininity" in little girls and discourage "tomboy" behavior. Parents as a rule don't know they practice this kind of discrimination because it is built so deeply into our culture. The growing boy or girl lives in a maelstrom of evaluation: praise or censure from Father and Mother, comments of relatives and neighbors, grades in school, and the judgment of peers. "Larry is athletic," they say. "Lucy is hopelessly shy." "Isn't it a shame about Nancy's hair!"

Parents can build into their children self-confidence and pride in who they are. But they can also create in their children a lifelong uneasiness with themselves. Some people have high morale and seem always to be happy with themselves, proud to be who they are. Others, known to be people of distinction and talent and charm, still have a deep sense that they are somehow inferior. How does this happen?

An example that occurs to me is that of a charming woman of Mexican ancestry who was brought up in Minnesota. There are not many Mexicans in Minnesota. Apparently her parents—especially the father—were extremely anxious about being accepted. He kept urging his wife and children to be more "American" and less Mexican. The girl was brought up, therefore, feeling that there was something wrong with being Mexican. It is understandable, however, how her father as head of the one-family minority had those feelings of insecurity which he passed on to his children.

The girl grew up to marry a tall, blond Scandinavian, handsome and reasonably successful in his profession. Her father was delighted with the marriage. One would have thought that she would be, too. But she cracked up. As psychotherapy eventually revealed, her good fortune proved almost intolerable. In her deepest emotion she felt, "Here am I, a Mexican, married to this wonderful, handsome man. Someone is going to tell him one of these days that I am a Mexican—and then I'll be thrown out." She lived in terror that she might be "found out." She is over it all now, but it was tragic to see her go through it. Everyone assured her, "You're beautiful and charming and just the ideal wife for Bob. He couldn't be luckier." But she couldn't really believe it inside.

What we do with children's self-concepts matters enormously in the long run. This is something that parents and teachers must never forget.

The Inequality of Men and Women

In an early issue of the women's liberation magazine *Ms.*, there appeared a model marriage contract, drawn up by Mrs. (or Ms.) Alix Shulman, allocating the mutual responsibilities of husband and wife. Here are a few sample clauses:

"Cooking: Breakfasts during the week are divided equally; husband does all weekend breakfasts (including shopping for them and dishes). Wife does all dinners except Sunday nights. . . .

"Cleaning: Husband does dishes Tuesday, Thursday, and Sunday. Wife does Monday, Wednesday, and Saturday. Friday is split according to who has done extra work during the week. . . .

"Laundry: . . . Wife does home laundry. Husband does drycleaning delivery and pickup. Wife strips beds, husband makes them."

Transportation of children to school or dentist and other chores are also equally divided in subsequent clauses.

The contract is prefaced with a statement that "we reject the notion that the work which brings in more money is more valuable. The ability to earn more money is a privilege. . . ."* Thus husbands may not be exempted from their share of domestic chores on the ground that they earn the family's livelihood. A man's work outside the home is not credited to his side of the ledger.

Obviously no such cut-and-dried arithmetic formula of domestic justice is going to resolve the dissatisfaction of housewives

* "How to Write Your Own Marriage Contract," *Ms.* magazine, Spring 1972, pp. 66–67.

or their husbands. Nevertheless, the fact that such a contract can be drawn up and proposed in all seriousness—a contract envious of men and their careers and resentful of homemaking and the burdens of motherhood—is a reflection of the severe frustrations in the lives of educated women as their roles are now defined in our culture.

Midge Decter, on the other hand, in *The New Chastity and Other Arguments Against Women's Liberation,* * does not believe that women are victims of male oppression. The present system, she believes, is as much a product of women's desires as of men's. According to Decter, women, especially in the social classes represented in the women's lib movement, are essentially parasites. For most married women, she says, work is a more frivolous venture than it can ever be for men:

"Married women work because it pleases them . . . to do so. They are free to earn less money if doing so provides them with an opportunity to do something more interesting or satisfying to them. They are free to leave a job whose conditions are not to their liking. They are free, that is, to continue to behave like dependents." Women, she says, are not deeply committed to their jobs. They are essentially volunteers. To a man, however, his job is of utmost importance; his career is his ultimate form of self-definition.

Women's liberation claims that men have a freedom denied to women—the freedom to escape the burdens of family in order to realize themselves in their careers. Decter says, on the contrary, that married women have a freedom denied to men—the freedom not to care, not to work. Which sex is the more oppressed, she asks—the men, who have to have careers, or women, who don't have to?

All this reminds me of something my daughter once said when she was about twelve years old. We were discussing the problems of her older brother. "It's easier being a girl," she said. "People expect so much of a boy."

For all the excesses of the rhetoric of much of the women's liberation movement, for all the Black Panther-like paranoia (for example, some speak of the role of the housewife as that of "house nigger"), for all the shrill hatred of males some express,

* New York: Coward, McCann & Geoghegan, 1972.

it appears to me that the movement touches on profound inequities in man-woman relationships.

"Jack," we say to our boys, "you've got to make something of yourself. You've got to realize your potential."

"Penny," we say to our daughters, "you've got to be sweet and charming so you will find a nice husband and find happiness in helping him realize his potential."

If Jack is a good mathematician or mechanic or debater, there is no limit to our aspirations for him. Maybe he'll grow up to be another Einstein, a Thomas Edison, President of the United States! But if Penny is a good mathematician or mechanic or debater, we hope that, despite these handicaps, she will grow up to be a good wife and mother.

Perhaps the ultimate devaluation of women is to expect little of them.

What's Wrong with Japanese Men?

According to a foreign journalist in Japan, Japanese women are rated No. 1 in admirable qualities, but Japanese men are twenty-sixth. "This tongue-in-cheek article," writes Jack Seward in *The Japanese*,* "incurred great wrath from two sources: (a) the Japanese men themselves, who felt that they had been unduly maligned, and (b) many foreign residents, who held that . . . a ranking of twenty-sixth place was outrageously high."

Jack Seward lived in Japan for twenty-five years and is married to a Japanese. He reads and writes the language. In this book he discusses the Japanese people, their customs, their language, their food and drink, their business practices, their religions, and their future in a thoroughly entertaining, highly personal, and therefore sometimes exasperating way. He has clearly been around a lot in Japan—in business conferences, in family meetings, in bars and geisha houses, in the little shops in the side streets off the side streets. He has seen Japanese plays and movies and watched television, understanding the dialogue—which is far more than I can do. I found it especially interesting to read his book during my last trip to Japan and to wonder to what extent he is right in his observations about Japanese people.

For example, Japanese men, says Seward, are lousy lovers. They are heirs of a samurai tradition that regards the expression of feelings of tenderness as a sign of weakness and effeminacy. Furthermore, a long tradition of male dominance has left women so docile and long-suffering, so quick to do what the lord-and-master wishes without protest or complaint, that men are spoiled rotten.

* New York: William Morrow, 1972.

As Seward describes it, there is little in the way of courtship in Japanese life. With marriage arranged by parents and go-betweens, a man can win a bride without having to court her. Love outside of marriage—which means with geisha, bar hostesses, or waitresses (whose job is to lure men back as well as to wait on tables)—also makes few demands on a man for the practice of the arts of courtly love, since it is the duty of such women to please the men rather than the other way around.

Seward describes a honeymoon couple as their train pulls out of the station, leaving congratulatory friends and weeping relatives behind. When the couple are alone at last, what next? "I have witnessed what usually happens many times," writes Seward.

"The bridegroom takes off his shoes and coat and hands the latter to his bride to fold neatly and place on the baggage rack above them. If the day is unseasonably hot, he may also take off his trousers, but not with any impatient thoughts of romance in mind.

"From his pocket he takes a transistor radio, switches it on and inserts the earplug. Next he opens a package of peanuts. If he is a kind soul, he may remember to offer some to his bride. Or he may hand her a tangerine—to peel for him. When he is . . . as comfortable as he can reasonably get, he buries his nose in a magazine and reads until he gets sleepy. When they reach the resort town where their marriage, born of passion, is to be consummated, he stands up and lets his wife help him on with his coat, then precedes her out of the coach. She meekly follows after him, carrying most of the luggage."

In short, Japanese men expect—and get—a lot of service. Taking all this attention for granted, they are thoughtless toward their wives and often rude and vulgar toward women in the service trades. And when they become affluent, they are likely to take on a mistress, and the wife is expected neither to complain nor to object.

How accurate are these generalizations about Japanese men? I certainly don't know, never having lived in Japan. But Japanese men can't be all that bad if, as Seward himself says, only one marriage in twenty-five in Japan ends in divorce while the figure for the United States is one in four.

But let me submit two other opinions. My sister, brought up

in Japan but now living near Detroit, also read the book while we were visiting in Yamanashi. She said, "On the subject of women, the author is at least a generation behind the times. I don't think he knows what's going on."

I also relayed Seward's conclusions about the lack of courtliness and tenderness in Japanese men to a twenty-four-year-old young man in Yamanashi. He agreed that Japanese men are not good at expressing tender sentiments. But, he added, "Things are changing fast. Already things are different from what they were in my generation."

"Your generation?" I asked, a little puzzled.

"Yes," he said. "The nineteen-year-olds are different from my generation. Boys have girl friends and are kind and thoughtful to them. Do you know why? Television commercials, showing boys and girls strolling hand in hand. They are giving young people a whole new way of looking at their relationships."

I was dumbfounded. I have always said that TV commercials are among the most revolutionary influences of our times. But sometimes the revolution takes quite an unexpected form!

How Do Boys Become Men?

Never has it been so difficult for boys to grow up into men.

Becoming a man is not a matter of chronology. It is a matter of proof. Throughout the history of mankind, boys have had to prove themselves men. Davy Crockett "killed him a b'ar when he was only three." Others, in order to establish themselves as men, have had to win races, prove their skill in hunting, show they could handle a team and plow, endure survival tests in the wilderness, bring home an enemy scalp, or drink half a pint of whiskey without passing out.

To become a man it has always been necessary for boys to associate with men—as helpers on their father's farm, as apprentices to craftsmen, as squires to knights, as waterboys to baseball teams. Through such association they learn the secrets of the adult culture: what rituals to observe, how to care for equipment, how to drink and curse and fight, how to earn and maintain the respect of other men in a society of men.

But today most boys are separated from the lives of men. Men leave for factory or office early in the morning, commuting many miles to work. They do not return until evening. Boys are brought up by mothers and schoolteachers. Hence boys often have no idea what their father does at work. They have no idea what a man does that makes him a man.

Unless a boy joins a street gang or is a good enough athlete to make the varsity squad, even if he joins the armed forces or goes to engineering school, he is likely to spend his entire life around women. Mobs of Radcliffe girls have invaded Harvard classrooms. Yale has gone coeducational. Girls move into fraternity houses. The experience of being a man in a society of men becomes rarer and rarer. It's fine for a boy to prove to women that he is a man. But the final proof is when he proves it to other men.

What young men profoundly need as they grow up, says David Riesman, is to be extended to the limit of their powers. They have to experience situations in which they have to do more than their best in order to escape death, capture, defeat, or failure.

But what is there in a boy's life in this affluent society to extend him to the limit of his powers? If he gets on the high school football team, he will really have to extend himself. But what of all the other students? High school is no challenge. In most communities if the student doesn't learn enough to go into the next grade, the school passes him anyway. For many the curriculum is so slow and repetitive that it is a bore. For others it is simply meaningless.

Furthermore, the challenges of work in the outside world are denied to the boy by exclusionary union rules, by child labor laws and, where these do not apply, by minimum wage laws, as well as by the legal and social pressures that keep him in school whether he wants to be there or not. So the vast majority of boys are excluded from the world of men and denied the chance to exercise their powers, physical or intellectual. Is it any wonder that there is a youth problem?

Boys need challenges. Their whole being cries out for them. To face starvation, the possibility of death at enemy hands, the risks of failure in school or work or business, and then to triumph over these dangers—these are the stuff of human growth, of maturation. If an affluent society does not provide boys with challenges, they are compelled by inner necessity to improvise their own. Is this not one of the reasons that gangs of youths try to provoke authorities into confrontations? Have you not observed the joy in their faces on learning that the police have been summoned? Have you ever seen such a need to assert manhood as was shown by the Black Panthers in the days of their heroics on televison?

What about drugs and the young? If challenge and risk are what so many youths need and are not getting, is it not likely that warnings about the dangers of drugs simply make them more attractive? And stealing cars! Whatever else a boy may be doing as he tears along the highway at 100 mph trying to evade the police, he is certainly extending himself to the limit of his powers. Youth gangs are societies of the young. Unlike the thirteen-year-old Pueblo boy who joins a khiva of male elders, the gang recruit joins a group almost as ignorant and inexperienced as himself.

That's what the generation gap is about: fathers away from home, for whatever reason, and therefore unavailable to their sons as models of male adulthood; the boys forced to improvise their own subculture, unguided by adult knowledge or experience. That's the problem for fathers. Isn't there something to be learned from the Pueblo Indians about passing on a culture? It takes men to make men. Mothers cannot do it by themselves. Nor can high schools. Nor colleges.

PART III

THE THEORY AND PRACTICE
OF YOU AND ME

The Four Uses of Language

The word-manipulating professions have of necessity grown in importance with increasing economic interdependency in a technological world. The more industrialized society becomes, the more carefully must human effort be coordinated—and this coordination is achieved through language. The result of this vast need for communication is familiar. The citizen of today, Christian or Jew or Muslim, financier or farmhand, stockbroker or stock boy, has to interpret more words per day than the citizen at any other time in world history.

Literate or semiliterate, we are assailed by words all day long: news commentators, soap operas, campaign speeches, newspapers, the propaganda of pressure groups or governments—all trying to sell us something, to manipulate our beliefs, whether about the kind of toothpaste to use or the kind of economic system to support. We are told these things sometimes for our own good, and sometimes for the good of those who tell us. We are living in a time when billions of dollars a day are spent by people who want to make up our minds for us.

It is natural that this kind of climate should generate widespread skepticism. Confronted by a thousand contradictory voices, we are tempted to say, "Let's not believe anybody." We have many skeptics in the modern world, people who simply refuse to believe anything. In my own experience, I have found that these skeptics belong to two large groups: first, those working people who tend to disbelieve newspapers, television commentators, and even the pronouncements of their own union leaders, and who believe, by and large, what they learn from face-to-face contact with people whom they have learned to trust. The second class of skeptics is found among those who themselves are in the word-manipulating profession. They have seen, or been party to, so many publicity stunts, planted news stories, political campaigns, "pseudo-events," and public relations drives, that they take a kind of professional pride in not believing anything.

Some academic people of my acquaintance are so clever that they see through everything: the logical weaknesses of the arguments for capitalism and against it; the weaknesses of the arguments of both theists and atheists; the shortcomings of science as well as of all the alternatives to science. These intellectual skeptics are perhaps in an even sadder state than the working-class skeptics, since the latter believe at least in each other as partners at work, and in the reality of their work. When a man builds a wall, he does not doubt the reality and validity of bricks. But the skeptic of the word-manipulating class is skeptical of the validity and worth of his own work, because if all communications are suspect, so are his own. This conviction leads to the kind of disintegration into cynicism not uncommon in the journalistic profession, in advertising, and (I am forced to admit) in politics.

It is in this situation that the science of semantics has arisen. It can help us find legitimate meaning among all the nonsense. Briefly stated, semantics is the study of relationships between words and things, between language and behavior, between language and reality. One of the basic questions of semantics is therefore what kinds of meaning language can convey. A helpful way of classifying the uses of language is to divide them into the following categories. First, there is the informative function, as in "The car is in the garage." The truth of an informative statement is to be found in looking beyond the words, into the garage, to see if the car is there. Second, there is language that is used to set up language: "A bachelor is an unmarried man." It isn't necessary to conduct a survey to find out how many bachelors are unmarried. Bachelors are unmarried by definition—which means by a rule of language. Third, there is the directive use of language. A statement like "no parking" or "one-way street" says nothing descriptive about the world. It merely tries to control the future behavior of motorists. Fourth, there is evaluative or expressive use of language, in which one expresses preferential feelings toward something or someone:

"You are the most beautiful girl in the world," or "The free enterprise system is the finest system on earth."

What is important is not to get the four uses of language mixed up.

Force as Communication

In the age-old question "How can people be made to agree?" two little words are commonly omitted that ought to be there. The question should read, "How can people be made to agree with me?" For we all have our convictions of rightness; almost by definition, the Peaceable Kingdom, in which the lion shall lie down with the lamb, is that happy condition in which all other people will have seen the error of their ways and accepted our views, our economic system, our religion, our politics.

Hence, underlying almost all our attempts to bring about agreement is the assumption that agreement is brought about by changing people's minds—other people's. "Wage earners must be made to see . . ." "Management has simply got to realize . . ." "The point must be made clear to the Russians . . ." "It's high time Susan understood . . ." Hence, too, the words we use to describe an agreement successfully arrived at are transitive verbs: I persuaded him, I convinced him, I educated him, I straightened him out, I cured him of his delusions. The almost invariable assumption is that somebody has to do something to the misguided individual in order to bring him to a realization of the truth. In the public relations profession, they used to talk about the "engineering of consent." Here, too, the same assumption is at work.

Let us examine this assumption more closely. The words we use to describe a successful act of communication are transitive verbs, which, as every schoolchild tries to avoid learning, are verbs with direct objects, as in:

The boy hit the ball.
The shoemaker mended the shoe.
The missionary converted the heathen.

In each of these statements the subject of the sentence (boy, shoemaker, missionary) remains unchanged—or at least nothing is implied about changes taking place. But great changes are produced in the object: The ball has traveled, the shoe has been modified and improved, the heathen are no longer heathen. According to the familiar implications of the transitive verb, the speaker is the active agent in an act of communication. The hearer is passive. He is the one to whom something is done.

The late Wendell Johnson of the University of Iowa used to say that there is a way in which "your language does your thinking for you." In thinking about communication, we tend unconsciously to take for granted the division of roles into those of the active speaker and the passive hearer. The commonest example of the transitive verb assumption in communication is that everyday occurrence of speech in which, having failed to communicate our wishes the first time, we raise our voice with each succeeding repetition:

Please close the door, son.
Will you *please* close the door!
DAMMIT, CLOSE THE DOOR!

And what if, after we have shouted at him several times, the little boy still won't close the door? What if, after repeated attempts to pierce the Iron Curtain with messages carrying assurances of our peaceful intentions, the Russians remain evasive and uncooperative?

The first thing that occurs to all of us, and the only thing that occurs to some of us, is to replace verbal force with physical force. Force, in other words, is regarded by most people as a technique of communication, a method of education. As the stern parent says, sparing neither rod nor child, "That will teach you a lesson!"

But when the purpose of communication is to bring about peace, a certain logical contradiction enters into such forceful methods of communication, persuasion—or education. It is the kind of contradiction the detached observer might point out on seeing a father spanking his son while saying to him, "This will teach you not to hit your little sister!" When the father himself becomes aware of the contradiction—and it sometimes happens (I speak autobiographically)—he is paralyzed with indecision. What does one do?

National bewilderment in the face of international tensions appears, then, to be understandable. We have inherited from the past a well-established pattern of how to behave when we want to change the attitude or behavior of others. The pattern is to start out with words, friendly, persuasive, cajoling, demanding, or commanding; then when we find we are getting nowhere, we raise our voice and intensify the vigor of our verbal efforts; then, when that doesn't work, we apply the threat of force; finally, force itself. But in international relations, we are confronted with a situation in which we are frightened (as well we might be) of taking the last step. We are also concerned with the logic (to say nothing of the morality and the practicality!) of starting a world war in order to prevent one.

Any pattern of behavior can be said to be deeply rooted if it cannot be changed even by experiences that clearly show its inadequacy. Such a deeply rooted but inadequate pattern of behavior is seen in the case of the wealthy playboy who, in the pursuit of happiness, marries an indefinite succession of attractive and avaricious blondes. Our customary pattern of behavior in the face of disagreement—the three-stage pattern of (1) gentle words, (2) stronger words, and (3) force—is likewise one that is not easily changed by experience.

Were it not for the fact that all the major (and many of the minor) nations of the world are busily engaged in strengthening their armaments, the following story would have little point. The story is that of Nick, the boy who is the central character in Willard Motley's tragic novel about the Chicago West Side, *Knock on Any Door.** Nick is in a death cell awaiting execution, convicted of the murder of a policeman after a long career of delinquency, reform school, and crime. Central in Nick's troubled career is his hatred and resentment of his father, whose educational methods can be inferred from his remarks on learning of his son's terrible fate. "I can't understand it," the father says; "I told him and I told him. And I always whipped him when he did wrong." Even when he is confronted with the disastrous results of his educational methods, it does not occur to Nick's father to question their rightness. He merely feels, as many fathers would, that he did the best he could—and therefore why did this have to happen to him?

* New York: D. Appleton-Century, 1947, p. 478.

The tragic irony of deeply rooted patterns of behavior is that their victims do not question their validity either. Nick's Aunt Rosa calls on him in his death cell. Nick asks:

"How's—Rosemary?"
"She's just fine—and that kid of hers—he's a cute one!"
Aunt Rosa took a long time between each answer.
"How's Junior?"
"Getting awfully big, Nick—and bad."
"Aunt Rosa—will you do me a favor?" Then embarrassed and staring at the toes of his shoes. Color deepened on his cheeks and he leaned forward before continuing. "Don't let him get too bad—don't let him end up like—*You beat the hell out of him, Aunt Rosa! You see that he does right.*"[Italics supplied.]

If Nick's advice is followed, what advice will Junior pass on from *his* death cell?

It Helps to Be Listened To

There are two aspects to communication. One is output—the speaking and writing. Most of the concern with communication is directed toward the improvement of the output. "How can I get people to listen to me? How can I convince them I'm right?" We find, therefore, on every hand, courses in communication, in effective speaking, in the arts of plain and fancy talk. But the other aspect of communication—the problem of how to listen well—is a relatively neglected subject. It does not avail a speaker to have spoken well if the listener has failed to understand, or if he believes the speaker to have said things he didn't say at all.

A common difficulty in conferences and committee meetings is what might be called the terminological tangle, in which discussion is stalemated by the fact that the parties concerned have different understandings of key terms. Someone says, "We need discipline in our schools." What does he mean? Perhaps he means that pupils should get more homework and harder tests. He may mean that they shouldn't run around and shout in the hallways. He may even mean that troublemakers should be horsewhipped and expelled. But if you assume you know what he means without listening further to him, you may well find yourself arguing over something he didn't say.

Or someone may say, "I think Senator Birch Bayh is a deeply conservative man." You can imagine how some people will react. "What? Birch Bayh? Conservative? Are you crazy?"

Terms like "conservative" and "liberal" and "progressive" and "reactionary" cannot be defined except in context. And even if the issue is known, the answer is not always easy. For example, Bayh, reputedly a liberal, voted against a foreign aid bill in the U.S. Senate, along with acknowledged conservatives like Senators Eastland and Stennis. Other known liberals like Senators Proxmire and Ribicoff voted for it, along with alleged conservatives like Allott of Colorado. If we can learn to delay our reactions when confronted with a statement like "Senator Bayh is a conservative," we will give ourselves a chance to learn something—whether about Senator Bayh or conservatism or the speaker.

Within the disciplined contexts of the sciences, exact or almost exact agreements about terminology can be established. But the words of general conversation and of political discussion are the language of everyday life—which means that words can mean many different things in different contexts. This fact is not to be either applauded or regretted. It is simply to be taken into account. And if we take it into account, we will be better listeners.

A good listener does not merely remain silent. He or she asks questions, carefully avoiding any tone of challenge or hostility. The questions must be motivated by a real interest in the speaker's views. These I call "questions for clarification." "Would you expand on that point about . . . ?" "Will you please restate your argument about . . . ?" Perhaps the most useful question is, "I am going to restate in my words what I think you mean. Then will you tell me if I've understood you correctly?"

There are also what I call "questions of uniqueness." All too often we listen to a speaker in terms of a generalization: "Oh, he's just another progressive educator . . . just another black militant . . . just another politician." Once we classify a speaker in this way, we stop listening because, we feel, "We've heard that stuff before." Questions of uniqueness prevent us from unconsciously denying the speaker a hearing. They take such forms as "How large is your school and what are your present disciplinary procedures?" "To what extent are the aims of your organization different from those of the Afro-American League?"

All too often the fact that misunderstandings exist is not apparent until deeper misunderstandings have accumulated in addition to the original one. We have all been at meetings at which Jones says something, Smith gives a heated response to what he mistakenly believes Jones said, and Jones tries to refute what he mistakenly believes Smith meant. In a matter of minutes the discussion is hopelessly mired in semantic quicksand, so that it may take anything from twenty minutes to two hours to untangle the mess. This is what happens when people discuss not for clarification, but for victory.

A good listener helps the speaker clarify—and often correct—his ideas in the course of expressing them. The young become good communicators if they have parents or relatives or teachers who are good listeners. A parent, therefore, is never wasting time when patiently listening to a child trying to explain something. Listening helps the child become an articulate—perhaps even an eloquent—adult.

Message and Metamessage

Two American men talk together comfortably at a distance of three or more feet from each other, unless, of course, they are forced closer by having adjacent seats in an airplane. Latin Americans are accustomed to shorter interaction distances—two feet or less. Therefore when an American and a Latin converse, the Latin tries to get closer in order to feel more comfortable. The American backs away—for the same reason. "I have observed an American backing up the entire length of a long corridor while a foreigner whom he considers pushy tries to catch up with him," writes the anthropologist Edward T. Hall in *The Silent Language,** a pioneer study of the differences between modes of nonverbal communication from one culture to another.

Studies of this kind were also much advanced by another anthropologist, Ray L. Birdwhistell, whose book, *Kinesics and Context: Essays on Body Motion Communication,*** brings together the results of years of study concerning how people communicate, their unstated wishes, their hidden hostilities, their unspoken appeals for attention or love, with eyes, facial expressions, and gestures of arms or legs or head.

I remember an evening with Birdwhistell and other friends in San Francisco many years ago, when he began expounding his theories about body communication, using as his example a pretty young English professor who was also a guest at the party. He had her figured out very well—why she was silent, why she crossed her legs and held her arms and shoulders as she did. He didn't miss very much about her except the fact that by the time he had finished his analysis, she was so angry that she would gladly have killed him!

* New York: Doubleday, 1959.
** Philadelphia: University of Pennsylvania Press, 1970.

Why, in our culture, is it impolite to stare? When you meet the eyes of a stranger in the street or on a bus, you are supposed to look quickly away. If your gaze lasts too long, it is likely to become embarrassing or annoying to the other person. In American cities if you look at a girl whom you do not know, she promptly averts her eyes. It was both a surprise and a pleasure to me, when I visited Norway, to find that when I looked at a pretty girl in the street, she would look right back—not provocatively or impudently, but simply in curiosity, like a child.

In a crowded New York subway, people read newspapers, stare out at the darkness, close their eyes. They don't look at each other. Nevertheless the eyes are the primary instrument of nonverbal communication. By gazing into each other's eyes, lovers assess each other's states of mind. We are suspicious of people who don't look us in the eye. We can tell by the movements of another's eyes whether he is happy, afraid, or just not listening. We avert our eyes to shield ourselves from an uncomfortable thought. Eyes can be aggressively impudent: "He undressed her with his eyes." They can be penetrating: "She saw right through me." They can be secretive, like those of a good poker player. Eyes narrowed and lowered can be seductive. Wide-open eyes express pleasure, surprise, disbelief.

Contact: The First Four Minutes by Leonard Zunin with Natalie Zunin* says that much, if not most, of what happens between people is determined by the first four minutes of interchange, and that while there are many kinds of verbal exchange by means of which people establish contact, the nonverbal interchanges are of enormous importance, both in giving meaning to what we say and in communicating what we are not ready to put into words.

A tilted head communicates curiosity—but with raised eyebrows or narrowed eyes signifies disbelief. Arms folded communicate a closed attitude, while spontaneous movements of the arms show openness. The shoulders reveal self-confidence or the lack of it. Hands, feet, or both jitter in impatience and nervousness.

In addition to all the nonverbal communication we apprehend by sight, there is communication by touch—something we all understood when we were babies in our mother's arms but which,

---

* Los Angeles: Nash Publishing, 1972.

after a long intellectualized education, most of us have to learn over again. Many of us learn through love and lovemaking; some learn through self-conscious training in tactile experience, as in the modern encounter group.

The Zunins tell us that the psychologist Sidney Jourard of the University of Florida observed couples in cafes in four different cities. "In Paris the average couple came into physical contact 110 times during an hour. In San Juan, Puerto Rico, couples patted, tickled and caressed 180 times during the same interval. But the typical London couple never touched at all, and Americans patted once or twice in an hour's conversation."

Are we in Anglo-American culture missing something?

What is comforting about "women's intuition" is that it is by no means exclusive to women. For example, two men meet and converse. As they leave each other, one says, "It was a pleasure meeting you." The other replies, "We must get together for lunch." As the result of such an exchange of courtesies, often the men do get together for lunch. But sometimes it is clearly understood by both parties that these words are merely stylized ways of saying, "Good-bye. I don't care if we never meet again."

How do we know when to believe what is said? We all make such interpretations intuitively, without analyzing how we go about it. When women make such interpretations accurately, men tend to attribute this to a special female power. But the process is not that mysterious. With every message (for example, "Let's have lunch"), there is a message about the message, technically called a "metamessage." The metamessage in this case may be the eagerness in the tone of voice, the cordiality of the handshake, the warmth of the smile, all of which say, "I mean it"—or the indifferent tone, the limp handshake and feeble smile, all of which say, "Forget it."

Many problems of communication revolve around the relations between message and metamessage. It is not enough to say what we mean. We have to sound and act as if we meant it. There has to be agreement or congruence between message and metamessage. If there is such congruence—if a person looks amused when he says amusing things, if he looks and acts angry when he says angry things—people may disagree with him, but they will not doubt his openness or sincerity.

This congruence is not, however, conclusive evidence of sincerity. Actors, for example, can read lines expressing love or jealousy with convincing expression without being in love or in a state of jealousy. Salesmen can express enthusiasm for a product without feeling any enthusiasm, except perhaps for making a sale. Most of us can put on an act when we have to. Nevertheless, we all tend to trust people in whom we find fairly regular congruence between message and metamessage.

The absence of congruence is readily noticed. There is the man who says, "I'm quite comfortable, thank you," as he shifts uneasily in his chair. There is the husband who says, "You know I love you," without lifting his eyes from the sports page. There is the schoolteacher who says, "I want you to be happy in this classroom," while her cold, watchful eyes contradict the smile on her lips. Sometimes communicative incongruence takes the form of complete lack of emotion in utterances that are normally impossible to say without feeling, such as, "I was never so happy in my life," or, "I hate him, I hate him."

All such profound incongruences are, to a greater or lesser degree, signs of emotional disorder, of something disconnected inside. Recently I read a case history of a woman in group therapy who was especially withdrawn and out of touch with reality. Suddenly something was said in that session that touched her. She sat upright, looked right and left with an expression of great alarm and said, "Where am I? Where am I? Is this some kind of nuthouse or something?" And that's exactly where she was—in a mental hospital. From her tone of voice and her expression of alarm, the psychiatrist knew at once that she had been reached—and from that moment she would start getting better.

Children are better than adults at understanding metamessages. As infants we do not understand words. We understand tones of voice, gentleness or harshness of touch, whether in love, irritation, or anger. Most of us, except the oververbalized and intellectualized, retain this understanding.

Women seem to be better than men at interpreting and responding to metamessages. When a man says at the end of a long, frustrating day, "I've had it. I'm going to quit this lousy job!" only an extraordinarily stupid or hostile wife would say, "Have you got another job lined up?" A concerned wife will say something like, "Why don't you take off your shoes and sit down while I get you a nice cold glass of Chablis?"

What is called "female intuition" is simply the greater sensitivity of women, due to their training, to metamessages, which are indicators of the emotional climate. So it's hard for parents to lie to children. It's hard for men to lie to women, too, but we all keep trying.

Language and Meaning

Semantics is concerned with how people talk. It is not concerned with the elegance of their pronunciation or the correctness of their grammar. Basically it is concerned with the adequacy of their language as a "map" of the "territory" of experience being talked about.

Here is a child playing in a living room. One observer says, "What a good child!" Another, who perhaps loves furniture better than children, says, "What an unruly child!" Neither of these statements gives a descriptive map of the territory of the child's behavior.

What are speakers talking about that they should arrive at such different perceptions? If they imagine they are actually talking about the child, there is immediate cause for dispute: Is the child well behaved or not? If the speakers understand from the beginning that they are each talking about the state of their own mind, that is something else again. Whether the differences in perception result in a quarrel and the breaking off of communications or in the further exchange of views, the outcome depends not only on what the speakers have said, but, more important, on their own attitudes toward what they have said.

There is an old story about three baseball umpires. One said, "I call 'em like they are." This view may be described philosophically as naive realism. The next said, "I call 'em like I see 'em." He may be described as a relativist, aware of the subjective element in any judgment. The third said, "They ain't nothing until I calls 'em." He is no grammarian, but he can be said to be a semanticist, deeply aware of the way in which the reality we live in is largely created by the language with which we describe it.

When semanticists talk about "language habits," they are referring to the entire complex: first, of how people talk—whether their language is specific or general, descriptive or inferential or judgmental; second, of people's attitudes toward their own utterances—whether dogmatic or open-minded, rigid or flexible.

Words are more than descriptions of experience. They are evaluations. How we think and evaluate are inextricably bound up with how we talk—not only to others but to ourselves. The behaviorist school of psychology asserts that all thought is subvocal speech. It is not necessary to go quite so far to concede the importance of this observation. Certainly most of thought is talking to ourselves silently. If spoken evaluations are hasty and ill-considered, unspoken ones are likely to be even more so.

A man says, "I don't like fish," although there are many, many kinds of fish and many, many ways of preparing them. But he still "doesn't like fish"—so that he even avoids clams and lobsters, which are no more related to fish than snails are to partridges. Perhaps the reader may think that this is a trivial example, but don't all prejudices—racial, ideological, religious, occupational—work in just this way?

"I don't like Russians."

"You know how taxi drivers are!"

"I can't stand women's clubs."

There are the ideologically muscle-bound who "don't like the profit system," whether it manifests itself in a corner newsstand or General Motors. Others reject "government intervention in business," no matter what kind of intervention in what kind of business for what purpose. Hence the unexamined key words in our thought processes, whether "fish" or "free enterprise" or "radicalism" or "the Establishment," can hinder and misdirect our thought by creating the illusion of meaning where no clear-cut meaning exists.

As the philosopher C. S. Peirce said, "It is terrible to see how a single unclear idea, a single formula without meaning, lurking in a young man's head, will sometimes act like an obstruction of inert matter in an artery, hindering the nutrition of the brain, and condemning its victim to pine away in the fullness of his vigor and in the midst of intellectual plenty."*

---

* Alfred Korzybski, *Science and Sanity: An Introduction to Non-Aristotelian Systems and General Semantics.* Lancaster, Pa.: Science Press Printing Co., 1933, p. 4.

Language, to be language, must have meaning. And meanings are not "out there." Meanings are semantic reactions that take place in people. A language is not simply sounds and spellings. It is the whole repertory of reactions that the sounds and spellings produce in those who speak and understand the language.

As Alfred Korzybski said, "A language, any language, has at its bottom certain metaphysics, which ascribe, consciously or unconsciously, some sort of structure to the world. . . . We do not realize what tremendous power the structure of an habitual language has. It is not an exaggeration to say that it enslaves us through the mechanism of semantic reactions and that the structure which a language exhibits . . . is automatically projected upon the world around us."*

And the task of education is not only to provide individual enlightenment but also to overthrow the tyranny of words by learning how to look beyond words to the complex realities for which they stand.

---

* Korzybski, "On Structure," Chapter IV, pp. 55–65.

The Threat of Clarity

The purpose of language is as much to conceal thought as to reveal it. Bureaucrats, high priests, lawyers, art critics, and other intellectuals develop a group jargon. The purpose of that jargon is only partly to communicate to other members of the group. An equally important purpose is to obscure or prevent communication to those outside the group.

It is easy enough to see that the underworld would want a secret language that outsiders cannot understand. People in the learned professions also have secrets to keep, especially from the lay public. It is not disputed that any learned profession requires a technical vocabulary. But such vocabularies almost always become more difficult than necessary. No physician has ever been able to explain to me the difference between "newborn" and "neonate."

The attractive fact about a learned vocabulary is that it confers social prestige and status upon its users at the same time as it creates awe among those who do not understand it. One of the pleasures of being learned is to induce in the unlearned the reaction, "God, he must be smart! I can't understand a word he says." And we who are learned are always just a bit afraid that if we were to express ourselves simply and clearly, people would cease to be impressed with us.

Historically, the intellectual's self-esteem has long rested on his conviction that he is of a special order of beings, far above the masses. "Some men are gold, some are silver, some are iron and lead," said Plato. Soldiers are silver. Artisans and workers are iron and lead. Philosophers are—guess.

Hence talking to each other in a language the masses cannot understand is a status symbol—almost a caste mark. In past ages intellectuals talked to each other in Latin or Sanskrit or classical Chinese, always making sure that these languages were no longer being spoken. These dead languages served the extremely useful function of keeping the peasants in a state of awestruck reverence before mysteries they could not hope to understand. The American scholar cannot, like his medieval counterpart, protect his exalted social image by writing in Latin. But he can and does write in languages almost as opaque. These words appear in a recent issue of the *American Journal of Sociology:*

"In any formal organization, the goals as reflected in the system of functional differentiation result in a distinctive pattern of role differentiation. In turn, role differentiation, whether viewed hierarchically or horizontally, leads to what Mannheim called 'perspectivistic thinking,' namely, incumbency in particular status induces a corresponding set of perceptions, attitudes and values."

What the author is saying in this passage is merely that different people have different jobs and that people in different jobs tend to see and think differently. (Read the passage over again and see if I'm not right.) This passage illustrates beautifully the dilemma of the ambitious American scholar. We who are scholars have to share findings with others. We have to communicate. As communicators we know from everyday experiences that the simpler and more unpretentious our vocabulary and syntax, the more quickly we are understood. But in addition to being scholars and communicators, we are status seekers, like everyone else. We want to impress others, if not with fine clothes or expensive automobiles, with the symbols of erudition. Therefore, relying on a tradition that goes back at least to the Chou dynasty in China, we work on the assumption that one can never be respected as a man of learning if everyone can understand what we say.

Ultimately we arrive at an uneasy compromise. We publish papers in order to communicate and thereby become members of the community of scholars. But we use a language that is guaranteed by its abstractness, its prolixity, and its utter lifelessness to discourage attention and to obscure comprehension. These observations can be stated as a general rule: *When the status-seeking functions of a learned vocabulary become more important to its user than its communicative function, communication suffers and jargon proliferates.*

Eschew Obfuscation

It often seems as if one of the rules of scholarly discourse in philosophy and the social sciences is never to use simple words if you can find learned and pretentious words to use instead. If you write so that everyone can understand, you are called a popularizer—or more likely, a mere popularizer. Friendly colleagues will say it more politely. Your views, they will say, are "simplistic and reductionistic."

On the other hand, if no one can understand what you write, your scholarly reputation becomes immense, like that of the German philosopher Hegel or the existentialist Martin Heidegger, and thousands of students from Heidelberg to Princeton to Berkeley to Bombay will bust their heads trying to understand you—many will even imagine that they do.

At any time in academic life there are words that become the vogue, as the word "parameter" is at present. "Parameter" is a mathematical term meaning "an arbitrary constant characterizing by each of its particular values some particular number of a system, as of expressions, curves, surfaces, functions" (*Webster's New International Dictionary,* 3d edition). There is a considerable jump from this technical definition to a usage such as this: "The curriculum in humanities must be designed within the parameters established by university policy." If you can substitute for "parameters" simpler words like "guidelines" or "limits," and the sentence makes better sense as a result, you can be sure the speaker is suffering from academic jargonitis.

The word "heuristic" means "aiding or guiding in discovery; designating an educational method by which a pupil is stimulated to make his own investigations and discoveries" (*Funk and Wagnalls Standard College Dictionary*). For example, one may properly say that a certain hypothesis, while unprovable, can serve as a heuristic tool. But "heuristic" has also become a jargon term through misuse and overuse as a kind of modest disclaimer, halfway taking back what one has just said: "I am merely offering this idea for heuristic purposes." This means, to translate it into another kind of jargon, "I'm just running it up the flagpole to see who salutes."

One day after reading five or six papers submitted to a social science journal on which I was serving as an editorial consultant, I decided to write a sociological paper of my own, observing all the rules of scholarly propriety. Here it is:

The Kallikaks and the San Francisco Giants: An Inquiry into the Formation of Attitudinal Sets
By S. I. Hayakawa, Ph.D.

On the basis of preliminary studies it would seem a reasonable hypothesis that among the situational factors predisposing the Kallikak family toward showing pronounced psychological identification with the San Francisco Giants over all other baseball teams is the fact that the Kallikaks make their domicile in San Francisco.

The Kallikaks' attitude in this respect would seem to confirm the findings of Glutzberg (1953, 1960) and the earlier researches of Platz (1947), which established that in the case of any given sports fan, his place of residence tends, within certain parameters yet to be conclusively defined, to correlate with his team preference.

In other words, San Franciscans who identify with the San Francisco Giants would seem to constitute an impressively large proportion of the baseball fans of that city. The same appears to be true of Cincinnatians, who tend to identify with the Cincinnati Reds. The situation in other National League cities has been touched upon (Kloepfer, 1965), but thorough studies have yet to be undertaken.

To return, however, to the Kallikaks, it would be going beyond the available evidence to suggest that their place of residence is the sole, or even the most important, factor determining their strong attitudinal set in preference for the Giants. Preliminary psychometric and sociometric studies of members of the Kallikak family disclose certain areas of atypicality which would suggest that other factors independent of place of residence may enter into the determination of their team preference.

The identification of these other factors, however, awaits the development of a conceptual framework adequate to deal with the full complexity of the intra- and interpersonal cultural and contextual variables involved.

What has been said here in three hundred words can be said, if you have "simplistic and reductionistic" habits of mind, in fewer than ten, thus: "People generally root for their hometown teams."

But why do we have to endure the academics and bureaucrats who insist on making verbal mountains out of intellectual molehills? How can people learn to think clearly, confronted with this onslaught of verbiage?

PART IV
EDUCATION: IS ANYBODY LISTENING?

How Education Takes Place

Human beings do not live simply to preserve life. They insist that life have meaning. And meaning is created and expressed by symbols, including not only symbols of church and nation, but language itself—the greatest and most complex of symbolic systems.

The fundamental motive of human behavior is not self-preservation, but the preservation of the symbolic self or self-concept. Self-concept is not the same thing as the self. It is an intellectual construct. It is your summary of what you mean to yourself as the result of all the thinking you have done about yourself, your experiences, your successes and failures, hopes and fears. It is your answer to the question, "Who am I?"

"I am a lady of fashion," you say, "I am a great business leader"—in which case you have to have that fur coat or that twentieth million. "I am a man of exceptional daring," you say, or "It is my mission to save the Japanese people from themselves by my heroic example"—in which case you have to climb Half Dome or commit harakiri. Every human being, says the psychologist Carl Rogers, is engaged in a lifelong process of trying to protect, maintain, and enhance his self-concept.

An English teacher, enthusiastically elucidating Shelley's "Ode to the West Wind," regards the ability to understand such a poem as essential to an educated mind. In teaching the poem he believes himself to be performing an important educational service. His student, however, with his own background, experience, and self-concept, takes a different view. To him Shelley's poem is a waste of time. Despite its revolutionary message, he may even regard it as a threat to his concept of himself as male, since his surrounding culture defines poetry as an unmasculine preoccupation.

The teacher urges the poem on the student for reasons that make sense to the teacher. The student resists for reasons that make sense to the student. "Everything we do seems reasonable and necessary at the time we are doing it," say Arthur Combs and Donald Snygg in one of the most understated but important principles in modern psychological literature.* The student's resistance to instruction in the appreciation of Shelley does not necessarily mean lack of intelligence. It may indicate strength of character.

The difficulties students have with mathematics usually have little to do with mathematical ability, but much to do with their self-concepts. If a girl defines herself as feminine and perceives mathematics as "unfeminine," she will resist mathematics for the same reason she refuses to wear lumberjack boots. Hence at the heart of a teacher's problems are problems of definition. How does the student define himself? What is his self-concept, and how does it affect the way he sees the world? How does the subject the teacher is teaching relate to the self-concept of the student? One of the skills of teaching is to get past the prejudices with which students often approach subjects they know nothing about. Stereotypes about which sex should be interested in what subjects are a pervasive form of mental slavery. Men as well as women need to free themselves from preconceptions if they are ever to realize their human potential.

Every school, every classroom needs an atmosphere of free communication. The teacher, by responding seriously and non-judgmentally to student comments, can free students from their fears of censure or ridicule and induce searching exploration of all points of view. He must also, by example as well as precept, teach the student who monopolizes discussion to be respectful of the views of all present, so that the student learns to listen as well as to talk.

An atmosphere of free communication means also that a teacher should feel free to lecture whenever the situation calls for the systematic presentation of a body of materials. The question here is not discussion sessions versus small groups versus

---

* *Individual Behavior.* New York: Harper & Brothers, 1949, p. 49.

lecture method. It is a matter of assuring by all means necessary the psychological freedom of all concerned, so that self-concepts can be relaxed, so that minds can be opened, so that intellectual growth and self-discovery can occur, so that self-discipline can take the place of adult admonition and guidance.

There is a sense in which it can be said that good teachers never really teach anything. What they do is to create the conditions under which learning takes place.

Why Some Children Cannot Spell

Some books you go back to again and again because they explain so much. One I reread often is Prescott Lecky's *Self-Consistency: A Theory of Personality,* published in 1945 and long out of print. Lecky died before his book appeared, and his name is rarely heard any longer in psychological circles. But what he wrote continues to stir my imagination.

What is the matter with the bright student who excels in all subjects, but cannot learn to spell? Lecky suggests an answer:

> This deficiency is not due to lack of ability, but rather to an active resistance which prevents him learning how to spell in spite of extra instruction. The resistance arises from the fact that at some time in the past the suggestion that he is a poor speller was accepted and incorporated into his definition of himself. . . .
>
> If he defines himself as a poor speller, the misspelling of a certain portion of the words he uses becomes for him a moral issue. He misspells words for the same reason that he refuses to be a thief.*

Are women inherently lacking in mathematical ability? Not if Lecky's theories are correct. Girls do just as well as boys in arithmetic in elementary school. But some time in high school girls are likely to be told that being good at math is "unfeminine," and at that point they are likely to develop an active resistance to learning any more algebra or geometry.

People's virtues and defects, Lecky said, are a matter of how they define themselves—what kind of self-concept they have. "I am a good cook," "I am a born salesman," "I am all woman," "I am a poor speller." Each element in the self-concept deter-

---

* New York: Island Press, p. 104.

mines the way in which the individual behaves—and develops. Prescott Lecky was an instructor in psychology at Columbia University from 1924 to 1934. He never received tenure or promotion. Because he had published little and never got his Ph.D., he lost his job and thereafter taught only part-time in the university's extension, supplementing his income with clinical practice.

Lecky's lack of success, professional and financial, was due in part to his theoretical opposition to the behaviorism prevalent during this period, especially in the psychology department at Columbia. It was also due to his unwillingness to publish anything he was not completely satisfied with. His lack of recognition and his poverty wore him down, so that at his untimely death in 1941 he left only two short published papers and a collection of manuscripts. However, Lecky had attracted a few gifted and extremely loyal students who were determined that his name be remembered. These included John F. A. Taylor, who brought Lecky's writings together in the book from which I quote.

Lecky was more favorably disposed toward psychoanalysis, which was very much the rage in his day, than to behaviorism. However, he felt that both schools of thought were in error in studying human behavior from the outside. He insisted that people must be understood from within. To understand an individual, it is necessary first to understand how he sees himself (his self-concept) and thus understand how he sees the world. It took the science of psychology a long time to arrive at the point that every good mother starts from.

And what about the boy who cannot spell? The answer lies in the word that is the title of Lecky's book, "self-consistency." Lecky believed that people need self-consistency. Finding contradictions in themselves, they are driven to solve them.

Most boys, Lecky explains, like to think of themselves as independent and self-reliant. But the poor speller "expects his defect to be condoned . . . he has his hand out, begging for indulgence. If the contradiction can be demonstrated from [the boy's] own viewpoint, a reorganization becomes compulsory. His definition of himself as a poor speller is vigorously rejected and a determined effort made to establish the opposite definition. The result is out of all proportion to the effort exerted to bring it about."

Lecky summarized his therapeutic method: "Instead of trying

to remove complexes, we try to change definitions." From "I am a poor speller," to "I am self-reliant in all respects, including spelling." From "I am no damn good," to "There are some things I can do well."

Changing self-definitions is not always easy. But Lecky's approach makes sense. Surely the discovery of one's own inconsistencies, with a psychologist's help or without, is the starting point of growth.

The Goals of Education

Basic goals of education are those that apply to everyone—men and women, the rich and the poor.

Goal One: To learn to understand, appreciate, and take care of the natural world we live in. Most people go through life unaware of the fascinating complex of events around them, of climate and terrain and vegetation and animals and people and their interrelatedness. Civilized people need to know not only what the environment is like, but how to keep it habitable.

Goal Two: To understand, appreciate, and learn to live with the fellow inhabitants of our planet. Every child must learn about the races and peoples of the world and the rich variety of the world's cultures. He must know something of the history of men and of nations. He must learn that there are many people in the world who differ profoundly in habits, ideas, and ways of life. He must perceive these differences not as occasions for uneasiness or hostility, but as challenges of his own capacity for understanding.

Goal Three: Every student should have an area of aesthetic experience—and I would include the religious and spiritual with the aesthetic. The aesthetic experience is the organization of our feelings—the search for and the creation of order in our affective life. The significances, the meanings that we perceive, are private. To give ourselves, for at least a part of the time, to the lonely contemplation of some kind of beauty and order is also to enrich ourselves so that we have something to contribute to the lives of others.

Goal Four: Everyone should be capable of earning a living. This can be learned in school or out, and at any level from humble work to highly paid, professional skills. Each of us needs to feel, sometime in life, that his services are important enough

97

so that someone other than the welfare department is willing to pay to keep him alive. Those who have never proved their usefulness remain forever at a disadvantage, because work is a basic way in which most of us relate to the world.

But work is, in a profound way, held in contempt by our educational system. Students believed to be low in academic talent are steered into vocational programs, while academically more gifted students are steered away from them, as if they were too good to be made to work. Such an arbitrary and invidious distinction inflicts an injustice both on the academically slow and on the advanced. All high schools and colleges should maintain an active relationship between the academic world and the world where people earn a living.

Goal Five: The last I regard as the most important of all— the learning of some kind of critical or intellectual method. We have all learned that we live in the age of an information explosion. But we are also in the middle of a misinformation explosion. With the proliferation of mass communications media, we are surrounded by hawkers, pitchmen, hard and soft sells, persuaders hidden and overt. Bombarded daily with millions of words by print and electronic media, we all have to have some kind of critical method by means of which to decide whom and what to believe, and to what degree.

How is propaganda evaluated? It cannot always be analyzed by scientific method, since propagandistic statements are rarely capable of proof; but it can be approached with a scientific attitude. Some kind of discipline in the orientations of science is necessary to inculcate a critical attitude toward words, our own as well as those of others, so that our lives may be governed by that skepticism and respect for fact that characterize the rational mind, though without the pervasive cynicism that disbelieves or doubts everything. We are living in a time when rationality has suddenly gone out of fashion. In the world of hip literary intellectuals, there are cults of mysticism; fads for such things as the I Ching, an ancient Chinese system of fortune-telling, divination by tarot cards, and astrology. The political left fostered a cult of violence, devoid of any serious social analysis, yet capable of producing followers cross-eyed with mindless fanaticism. Never has rationality been so badly needed as in this period when intellectuals themselves are spearheading the drive toward anti-intellectualism.

Active and Energetic Learning

One of the great superstitions about education is that learning is the result of teaching. Of course it often is. But an enormous amount of learning goes on without a teacher or parent present. Children learn much by imitating others. Young ones learn what to avoid by watching what their older brothers and sisters get punished for. People do not always learn from experience, but they certainly learn by reflecting upon their experience.

Wanting to learn is the most important ingredient of the learning process. I think of the way my own boy learned as a teenager to take apart and put together an automobile. I never could have taught him. He didn't take a course in high school in auto mechanics either, since he was verbally gifted and therefore steered into an "academic" rather than a "vocational" program. (There's that caste system for you!) But Alan wanted to know about automobiles. So he hung around garages, helped out at service stations, rummaged for parts in auto-wrecking yards. In the course of a year he picked up an amazing amount of information—and skill. He found his own instructors among mechanics, body-and-fender men, used-car salesmen, parts dealers. He organized his learning for himself.

Learning is an extraordinarily active process. When you see the energy and enthusiasm with which young people acquire knowledge—especially about things you don't want them to learn—you cannot help being impressed by their learning ability.

Since learning is an active process, it is sometimes likely to be noisy. I am told that there are public schools in which principals walk down the corridors to listen to the noise level in the classes. If there is a lot of noise going on in Room 5, where Miss Wilcox is in charge, Miss Wilcox is likely to be in trouble. She will be told that she is "not able to maintain discipline."

The idea behind this is the ancient motto, "A good classroom is a quiet classroom." I would amend this to say that a quiet classroom is a good prison camp.

Teachers often say that students should be encouraged to think for themselves. But they are usually given no such encouragement. Often students are concerned chiefly with learning what answers the teacher wants on the final exam. But supposing teachers really encouraged students to think for themselves? There would be no "right" answers to enormously important questions. What were the causes of the Civil War? Of the Japanese attack on Pearl Harbor? What were the beneficial and harmful effects of the Wagner Act? What did George Herbert Mead mean by the "generalized other"? The more freely students disagree among themselves, the more they have to know to back up their side of the dispute—and the more they read on their own, stimulated not by a teacher's requirements but by the demand of their peers before whom they must defend their position.

All this reminds me of the University of Chicago Laboratory School as it existed more than twenty-five years ago, when Alan was in kindergarten during the last year in which Miss Olga Adams, a disciple of John Dewey, was a teacher there. Because it was a famous laboratory school there were many visitors, most of whom were appalled initially at the noisiness of the situation. That huge room with dozens and dozens of children running around and shouting at each other seemed to be a condition of total anarchy.

But those who remained to observe learned that the situation was far from anarchic. Children were working on projects, going from one part of the room to another to get equipment or supplies, often running all the way in their enthusiasm. Others were calling out instructions to each other as they worked. Some children were reading aloud to others. Some were singing. Assistant teachers in sufficient numbers were always there to know exactly what was going on. There were periods of quiet, too—time for thought, for reflection, for calmness. But, Miss Adams warned, enforced quietness too often means not silent reflection, but boredom.

In kindergarten, as in the university, there should be a cardinal rule of education: Don't let your students get bored. And if you are a teacher and bored yourself, for your sake as well as for the children's sake, take a leave of absence to refresh yourself—or resign.

One Tuesday while I was lunching at the faculty club, a young professor of psychology began hesitantly to tell me of something that had happened in his class. "Sunday night," he told me, "I went to a big, drunken party. I went to my Monday morning class with a huge hangover."

"Then?" I asked sympathetically.

"Well, I told the class I had a hangover and was not prepared to lecture. Then I invited them to discuss the course in any way they wanted, and I would try to help the discussion." The professor continued with a troubled sigh. "Do you know," he continued, "that we had the best class discussion of my entire teaching experience? They asked questions that had never occurred to me. I was forced to do some quick thinking, relating my psychological knowledge to their questions. How, they asked, did my psychological theories apply to such-and-such a current political problem? To explaining such-and-such a rock musician's recent suicide? To analyzing the motivations and plot of such-and-such a currently popular movie?

"And when we got through," the professor concluded, "I think both my students and I understood better the meaning of the psychology I am trying to teach them."

I refrained from suggesting that he turn up with a hangover for every class meeting. However, I could not help thinking about the implications of his experience. He was ashamed of himself for not having a lecture prepared for that Monday morning. And he was startled that the session had turned out so well nevertheless.

Why had it? Because, many modern teachers will tell you, the professor's class, which had been overstructured by his elaborate daily preparations, benefited greatly when there was a change to an unstructured situation that created an opening for two-way communication and unplanned developments.

On the other hand, one can go too far in the direction of the "unstructured classroom." Some teachers, deciding that lecturing is an authoritarian practice, gave it up entirely and made a point of going to classes entirely unprepared, ready for everything—or nothing. Many also stopped using textbooks, giving reading lists, demanding term papers or final examinations. When my son took freshman English at San Francisco State some years ago, he was not required to write a single composition or take an exam. But he got an A—as did everyone else in the class.

For a while, especially in the late 1960s, the college had scores of hip young instructors who turned their classrooms into encounter groups, amateur therapy sessions, exercises in sensory awareness, and the like. One went to class not for knowledge, not for intellectual discipline, but to "groove." And these hip instructors attracted hundreds of students uninterested in studying. That was a big part of the trouble in the period of college turmoil.

I was not unaffected by the new approaches to teaching that swept through education in the 1960s. I too began an experiment with an adult evening class of thirty. At the beginning of the semester I assigned students their reading and told them what papers they were expected to write. After that I started each evening not with a lecture but with an invitation to discussion, "What's on your mind tonight?" And whenever questions or problems were raised, I refrained from giving answers. I simply tried to restate and clarify the question, then throw it back to the rest of the class—who soon found themselves talking to each other more than to me. After some thirty or forty minutes of this, I broke up the class into five groups of six ("buzz groups") to explore their problems further. In these small groups all who were too shy to speak before the whole class found themselves able to join the discussion. While the buzz groups met for another thirty or forty minutes, I withdrew to my office.

My lectures occupied the last part of the evening—not lectures prepared in advance, but directly in response to the questions raised by the students in their earlier discussions. Sometimes I would have to say to a question, "I haven't an answer now, but I'll try to have one by next week." But no one slept through my lectures, because I was talking about what they themselves had asked.

The traditional argument against student-directed classes is that the material is not likely to be covered unless the professor goes over it with them. I discovered at the end of the term that the students knew the material very well. They had read the books. Many technical terms I had never defined or discussed in class were used correctly and with understanding in their final papers and exams. What struck me most about this class was that after the course was over, the people in it kept having parties once a month for over a year because they missed each other. I missed them too. Some of my best students in general semantics came out of that course.

What Does It Mean to Be Creative?

What distinguishes the creative person? By creative person I don't mean only the great painter or poet or musician. I also want to include the creative housewife, teacher, warehouseman, sales manager—anyone who is able to break through habitual routines and invent new solutions to old problems, solutions that strike people with their appropriateness as well as originality, so that they say, "Why didn't I think of that?"

A creative person, first, is not limited in his thinking to "what everyone knows." "Everyone knows" that trees are green. The creative artist is able to see that in certain lights some trees look blue or purple or yellow. The creative person looks at the world with his or her own eyes, not with the eyes of others. The creative individual also knows his or her own feelings better than the average person. Most people don't know the answer to the question, "How are you? How do you feel?" The reason they don't know is that they are so busy feeling what they are supposed to feel, thinking what they are supposed to think, that they never get down to examining their own deepest feelings.

"How did you like the play?" "Oh, it was a fine play. It was well reviewed in *The New Yorker.*"

With authority figures like drama critics and book reviewers and teachers and professors telling us what to think and how to feel, many of us are busy playing roles, fulfilling other people's expectations. As Republicans, we think what other Republicans think. As Catholics, we think what other Catholics think. And so on. Not many of us ask ourselves, "How do I feel? What do I think?"—and wait for answers.

Another characteristic of the creative person is that he is able to entertain and play with ideas that the average person may regard as silly, mistaken, or downright dangerous. All new ideas sound foolish at first, because they are new. (In the early days of the railroad, it was argued that speeds of twenty-five mph or over were impractical because people's brains would burst.) A person who is afraid of being laughed at or disapproved of for having "foolish" or "unsound" ideas will have the satisfaction of having everyone agree with him, but he will never be creative, because creativity means being willing to take a chance—to go out on a limb.

The person who would be creative must be able to endure loneliness—even ridicule. If he has a great and original idea that others are not yet ready to accept, there will be long periods of loneliness. There will be times when his friends and relatives think he is crazy, and he'll begin to wonder if they are right. A genuinely creative person, believing in his creation, is able to endure this loneliness—for years if necessary.

Another trait of the creative person is idle curiosity. Such a person asks questions, reads books, conducts investigations into matters apparently unrelated to job or profession—just for the fun of knowing. It is from these apparently unrelated sources that brilliant ideas often emerge to enrich one's own field of work.

Finally, the creative person plays hunches. "Pure intellect," says Dr. Hans Selye, the great medical researcher at the University of Montreal, "is largely a quality of the middle-class mind. The lowliest hooligan and the greatest creator in the fields of science are activated mainly by imponderable instincts and emotions, especially faith. Curiously, even scientific research, the most intellectual creative effort of which man is capable, is no exception in this respect."*

Alfred Korzybski also understood well the role of undefinable emotions in the creative life. He wrote, "Creative scientists know very well from observation of themselves that all creative work starts as a feeling, inclination, suspicion, intuition, hunch, or some other nonverbal affective state, which only at a later date, after a sort of nursing, takes the shape of verbal expression worked out later in a rationalized, coherent . . . theory."**

* Hans Selye, *The Stress of Life.* New York: McGraw-Hill, 1956, p. 34.
** Korzybski, p. 22.

Creativity is the act of bringing something new into the world, whether a symphony, a novel, an improved layout for a supermarket, a new and unexpected casserole dish. It is based first on communication with oneself, then testing that communication with experience and the realities one has to contend with. The result is the highest, most exciting kind of learning.

PART V
THE MEDIA: ONE-WAY COMMUNICATION

Who's Bringing Up Your Children?

The semantic environment is the verbally and symbolically created environment in which all human beings live. It is the environment of news, information, beliefs, attitudes, laws, and cultural imperatives that constitute your verbal world. A quick way of describing the semantic environment is to say that it is that part of the total environment one's pet dog, lying on the rug, has no inkling of. Dogs do not grasp the world of Shakespeare and Mozart and Bugs Bunny and the Beatles; of Moses and Jesus and Billy Graham; of published batting averages and closing prices on the New York Stock Exchange; of news from Tokyo and Prague and Kinshasa. The semantic environment is the product of that vast network of communication we call civilization.

In a way we all share a common semantic environment—one created by the major news services, networks, and the intellectual climate of our times. In another way, each of us inhabits a semantic environment not quite like that of anyone else, since all of us read different magazines and books, listen to different speakers, watch different TV shows, hear different information and rumors at different places of work. Some were brought up in Catholic homes, some in Protestant; some read art journals or sports car magazines and others do not.

For most of the history of the human race, the semantic environment of children has been created by their parents and close relatives, who pass on to the young their pictures of the world, their value systems, their standards of behavior. As the children grow older, their semantic environment is expanded by other influences: friends, neighbors, movies, and the experience of school. Schools continue the process parents have begun; as a rule parents want their children to "do well" in school, which

109

means to absorb faithfully the messages directed at them by the educational system. The semantic environment of children is never altogether the same as that of their parents, whose minds were formed at another time under other influences. Nevertheless, there is normally some continuity between generations because of a background of shared communications and shared values—and this is true even in immigrant families in which parents speak an Old World mother tongue and the children speak English.

This process of time-binding by which parents play an important role in shaping their children's ideas and values has been going on for perhaps the whole history of the human race. We take the process so much for granted that few of us have awakened to the fact that, for millions and millions of families, especially in the United States, it just isn't taking place anymore.

Suppose from the time that children are old enough to sit up, they are snatched away from their parents for three or four or more hours a day by a powerful sorcerer. This sorcerer is a storyteller and a spinner of dreams. He plays enchanting music; he is an unfailingly entertaining companion. He makes the children laugh; he teaches them jingles to sing; he is constantly suggesting good things to eat and wonderful toys for their parents to buy them. Day after day, month after month, year after year, children for a few hours a day live in the wonderful world created by the sorcerer—a world sometimes frightening, often fun, and always entrancing.

The children grow older, still under the sorcerer's daily spell. The children find parents and relatives and teachers sometimes censorious, often dull, but the sorcerer never. They sit before him as if drugged, absorbing messages that parents did not originate and often do not even know about. For as much as one half or more of their waking hours from infancy onward, they live in a semantic environment their parents did not create and make no attempt to control.*

* "Children get more verbal impact from radio and television than from parents, teachers, neighbors and church combined. . . . By the time he enters first grade, the average child has spent more hours in front of the television set than he will spend in a college classroom." Nicholas Johnson in the Washington *Post,* June 16, 1968.

"A recent study by the Carnegie Corporation, the Ford Foundation, and the

The present generation of young people is the first in history to have grown up in the television age. A parent born in 1938 was ten years old in 1948 and had already lived through his most important formative years, so that in all likelihood he missed the experience of having a television set for a baby-sitter. But a significant proportion of children born after 1945, brought up in their parents' homes, to be sure, had their imaginative lives, their daydreams, their expectations of the world created by television. Is it any wonder that these children, as they grew to adolescence, often turned out to be complete strangers to their dismayed parents?

The impact of television is due in part to the nature of the medium, in part to the fact that American television is commercially sponsored. This last fact is of tremendous importance, despite Marshall McLuhan's famous dictum "The medium is the message." I hasten to acknowledge the important point that Professor McLuhan makes about television's influence in shaping our sense of the world through shaping our perceptual habits and our time sense. But to accept his pronouncement too literally is to say in effect, "Programming doesn't matter. Bad programs have the same effect as good. Programs whose only intent is to sell beer or automobiles are not different in their effect from religious programs, news programs, political education programs. The medium *is* the message." I do not believe Professor McLuhan's view can be accepted. If the messages of American television were overwhelmingly sponsored, say, by churches and universities instead of by advertisers of consumer goods, would its effects be no different from what they are now?

An important fact about television—regardless of its sponsorship—is that there can be no interaction with it. A child sitting in front of a television set gets no experience in influencing behavior and being influenced in return. Having a puppy is in this sense far more important to a child than having a television set, although of course there is no reason a child should not have both. The child who watches television for four hours daily

U.S. Office of Education found that preschool youngsters spend 54.1 hours a week watching television." Walker Sandbach, executive director of Consumers Union, Inc., in a speech before the Telecommunications Symposium of the Broadcast Advertising Club of Chicago, March 29, 1968.

between the ages of three and eighteen spends something like 22,000 hours in passive contemplation of the screen—hours stolen from the time needed to learn to relate to siblings, playmates, parents, grandfathers, or strangers. Is there any connection between this fact and the sudden appearance in the past few years of an enormous number of young people from educated and middle-class families who find it difficult or impossible to relate to anybody—and therefore drop out?

These young people are boys and girls who are frightened of the ordeal of having to make conversation with their friends' parents or anyone else not of their immediate clique. Many of them communicate, if at all, in monosyllables. Some merely grunt. The task of relating to others is found so threatening and burdensome that some have gone so far as to establish a Sexual Freedom League, in order to justify copulation without communication.

Can anyone doubt the enormous greed for consumer goods that was revealed in every outbreak of looting and civil disturbance since Watts? The disorders in Detroit in the summer of 1967 were characterized by a lack of racist motivation in many of the looters. Whites helped blacks and blacks helped whites load up their cars with expensive television sets, furniture, and luggage—all in a spirit of interracial brotherhood. We read that a gay, carnival spirit attended the looting. One Detroit newspaperman said the outbreak was simply an explosive response to color television. Furthermore, in order to attract larger audiences than the next network, all networks have glorified violence to a degree almost impossible to believe for those who are at all selective in their viewing. As Fredric Wertham has said in *A Sign for Cain*, "Violence on the screen is depicted as a way of life. Few arguments or conflicts on TV are settled without a fight. Never, literally never, is it taught in this School of Violence that violence in itself is something reprehensible. . . . No one can understand the world of today if he does not know what we put and permit on the airwaves. We are hypocritically surprised when young people in the slums fight the police. On the screen . . . the sport of killing policemen flourishes. . . . Police brutality is also graphically displayed."*

* New York: Macmillan, 1956; see Chapter X, "Mayhem in the Mass Media."

The militancy of the radical young—both white and black—eager for social change is often accounted for by saying that they have lost faith in the slow processes of democratic discussion and decision making. This argument seems highly questionable. It is my impression that militant young people, far from being "disillusioned" with democratic processes, are totally unacquainted with them, since they are rarely shown on television.

The unfamiliarity of young people with democratic processes is illustrated by the history of the "teach-in." It is a source of both pride and embarrassment to me that the "teach-in" was invented at my home some summers ago by a group of scholars then serving as fellows at the Center for the Advanced Study of Behavioral Sciences at Palo Alto. The original idea was that teachers of every shade of opinion about the war in Vietnam would give their views, so that everyone, especially students, would be better informed about the history of the conflict and the possible solutions. But the original idea was never given a chance. The proposal of the teach-in as debate was scuttled by the youthful organizers (and the middle-aged adolescents who were their faculty advisers) in favor of the teach-in as demonstration. Consequently, from the very first teach-ins at Ann Arbor and Berkeley, speakers defending the American intervention in Vietnam were hooted down. People came to meetings equipped not with lecture notes on Southeast Asian history, but with guitars.

If young people did not learn of the complexities of the democratic process from their years of viewing television, what did they learn? They learned that social problems are never complicated; they are simply the conflicts between good guys and bad guys. Bad guys can never be reasoned with—you can only shoot it out with them. If the bad guys confront you with superior force, you can lay your body on the line and go down fighting.

Young people learned from commercials that there is an instant, simple solution to all problems: Acid indigestion can be relieved with Alka-Seltzer; unpopularity can be overcome by using Breck shampoo; feelings of sexual inadequacy can be banished by buying a new Mustang, which will transform you into an instant Casanova.

Television documentaries about the problems of the world offer neat, half-hour wrap-ups of complex events. Highlights are selected, while boring, tedious details are left out. Time is compressed; cause and effect are simplified. In most situation dramas, people are presented not in the full complexity of their humanity, like people in real life, but in stereotyped roles. They arrive at their emotional responses quickly and easily, each Pyramus to his Thisbe, each Harlequin to his Columbine. In private as in public affairs, life is not too hard to understand. That's what television says.

But, as general semanticists are fond of saying, the map is not the territory. All too soon, young people learn that the maps of reality given them by television do not correspond to the actualities. Material possessions and the consumption of all approved national brands do not bring happiness or peace of mind. The world, they discover as they approach adulthood, is far more complicated than they ever suspected. Getting along with other people is not easy: You have to adjust to them as much as they have to adjust to you. The world makes all sorts of demands that the television set never mentioned, such as the necessity of study, hard work, patience, a sense of responsibility, a long apprenticeship in a trade or profession, and striving for advancement, before what the world has to offer can be enjoyed.

Disillusioned young people may rebel against the culture and its "materialism," not realizing that what they are rejecting is not the culture as such, but merely the culture as depicted by Madison Avenue and the networks. Even as they reject the culture as they understand it through television, they miss the pleasant fantasies they enjoyed as children when they turned on the set. So they "turn on" in other ways. Having scornfully rejected the notion that they can achieve instant beauty and radiance with Clairol, they espouse the alternative view that they can achieve instant spiritual insight and salvation with drugs. The kinship of the drug experience with television is glaringly obvious: Both depend upon "turning on" and passively waiting for something beautiful to happen.

What I have presented may seem like a terrible condemnation of television. It is not intended as such. Television is a wonderful instrument of communication, perhaps more effective than any in the history of the world. As Nicholas Johnson says, it is absurd to try to draw a line between "educational television" and "entertainment." All television is educational.* All television programs tell us something about the world, shape our expectations and hopes. The messages of television, with words reinforced by music and pictures and action, received in a darkened room in the privacy of one's home, reiterated over and over for those who view it daily, are the most powerful and effective communications ever let loose on the world; they affect millions of families day after day, night after night, every day of the year.

Because television was invented at a particular time, in a particular state of our economy, it was assigned almost entirely to utilization for commercial purposes. This decision was made in ignorance of the possible consequences—an entirely pardonable ignorance, since no one knew at the time what the social impact of this new medium might be. Business and the advertising profession are not to be blamed for making use of this medium as energetically and ingeniously as possible. There are no villains in this story; we are all simply victims of the unforeseen consequences of a technological revolution—and a revolution in the technologies of communication always has more far-reaching consequences than anyone can predict.

I am not pleading for more "quality" programming in the manner of many intellectual critics of television. Television is a mass medium. Half the people of America (as a brilliant statistician once pointed out) are of less than average intelligence and they have as much right to entertainment and instruction by television as the other half. What I am asking is that we give thought to how television might be financed otherwise than by advertising and therefore actuated by motives other than those of salesmanship, direct or indirect. Our national problem is not that we have commercial television, but that we have it almost to the exclusion of all other possible kinds. Is it not possible to get a more balanced choice of alternatives in television fare than we are now getting?

The problems raised here deeply involve students of child development. What kinds of programs are good for children—and at what ages? Does the excessive viewing of television, as many of us suspect but few of us can prove, result in fantasy

* *How to Talk Back to Your Television Set.* Boston: Atlantic–Little, Brown, 1970; See Chapter I, "The Crush of Television."

living, poor study habits, and alienation? There are problems too for students of literature. Delmore Schwartz said, "In dreams begin responsibilities." The imaginative representations of life, as depicted by commercial television, are a form of literature, shaping people's daydreams and life-styles, just as surely as *The Song of Roland* or *Huckleberry Finn.* What models of conduct does present-day television programming hold up for the young to emulate? What dreams of future achievement or success does it generate in boys and girls to direct their energies and aspiration?

I don't imagine there is a shred of evidence, other than subjective and intuitive, to support a theory about television's effect on the state of mind of youth today. The trouble is that what research there is on the effects of television is for the most part limited to research by advertising agencies on the effectiveness of their campaigns. Inquiries into the overall effects of television—on politics, on public opinion and decision making, on the life-style of young people and the psychic lives of young children—are only beginning.

Advertising as the Imitation of Art

Aldous Huxley once wrote, "Advertising is one of the most interesting and difficult of modern literary forms." He was certainly right. For some time it's been running through my mind that what advertising communicates and what poetry communicates are very much allied to each other. To be sure, poetry is generally understood to be something very special, to be studied in school, to be read aloud on solemn occasions, to be enjoyed by cultivated people; whereas advertising is part of everyday life. But let me point to some of the similarities between the two arts. At the obvious level, both poetry and advertising make use of rhyme, rhythm, and of words chosen for their connotative rather than their denotative value. The rhyme and rhythm are evident in every singing commercial.

To choose just one example of connotation as opposed to denotation in words, consider the advertisement for Di-Gel that says it is an effective remedy for acid stomach because it contains "simethicone." Neither you nor I (unless you are a chemist) know what "simethicone" is. And that's exactly why they continue to talk about it. Because we don't understand the word, we are led to believe that it is something magical and wonderful, like "RD-119," which makes motor oils so much more effective. Effective communication in advertising often means that no facts are communicated—only suggestions of magic, wonder, and delight.

Poetry seeks ambiguity—overtones of meaning that continue to haunt the mind, like Tennyson's "God made himself an awful rose of dawn." Advertising also thrives on ambiguity. "Clear heads choose Calverts." There are at least two meanings to "clear heads." Smirnoff's vodka "leaves you breathless." Breathless with delight? Or with a breath that does not reveal that you have been drinking? Or both?

William Wordsworth, in one of his poems about rural life, described a clodlike peasant mentality in the following words: "A primrose by the river's brim, A yellow primrose was to him, And it was nothing more."* To that poor fellow, a primrose was nothing but a primrose. The man had no poetic imagination. To a poet the primrose could be a symbol for his love of Lucy, an evidence of the beauties of England in springtime, a mark of the benevolence of God—or whatever he wanted to make of the primrose. The fellow, not being a poet, would not have made a good advertising copywriter either. The copywriter, if he had to advertise primroses, would make them symbolic of youth, gaiety, and good times, like Pepsi-Cola; or of romance and aristocratic elegance, like the Helena Rubinstein line of cosmetics; or of solid, traditional American virtues, like Old Crow. In other words, the writing of advertising is very much a matter of poeticizing consumer goods.

With pictures and with copy, advertising casts an imaginative glow over otherwise commonplace items: Marlboro cigarettes suggest the free-spirited cowboys of the West, "in Marlboro country, where the flavor is"; Schlitz beer emphasizes the life lived with gusto; Salems suggest not the agonies of lung cancer, but the magic of sparkling brooks and budding trees in springtime; Wheaties, which used to be "the breakfast of champions," are now connected with thoughts of adventure in outer space; the Datsun, like the Emancipation Proclamation, "sets you free."

Poetry and advertising are alike, too, in inviting the reader to put himself into a role different from that to which he is accustomed. When you read "Horatius at the Bridge," you are for the time being, in imagination, a brave Roman soldier fighting off the barbarians. Likewise when you read *Playboy* (advertising or text or both), you are for the time being the sophisticated, pleasure-seeking, well-to-do man-about-town, with an enlightened connoisseurship about sports cars, wines and liquors, and women.

Oscar Wilde once said, in a moment of extreme flippancy

---

* From "Peter Bell: A Tale," in *Selected Poems of William Wordsworth*. London: Oxford University Press, 1932, p. 218.

or remarkable wisdom, "Life is an imitation of art." The more I have thought about this aphorism, the more profound it seems to be, because poetry and drama and the novel and movies and advertising exact of us the tribute of imitation. And insofar as they do so, they are all "creative" arts. When I was a young English instructor, I used to think it pretentious and absurd of advertising agencies to refer to their art and copy producers as the "creative division" of their companies. I do not think so any longer. Movies, TV shows, popular music, and advertising all enter into our imaginations, and therefore affect our clothes, our attitudes, and ultimately our life-styles. Life is indeed an imitation of art.

Said Alfred Korzybski, "Human beings are a symbolic class of life. Those who rule our symbols rule us." Advertisers, newsmen, novelists, moviemakers, and others who create and manipulate our symbols are a ruling class whether they know it or not.

The Spoken, the Written, and the Printed Word

There are many ways in which societies accumulate and transmit knowledge. Primitive (or preliterate) societies depend on human memory for the storage of knowledge and on the human voice for its transmission. Primitive people usually have powerful memories, since they cannot write things down in notebooks for later reference.

Alex Haley tells in *Roots** his amazing story of his search for his African ancestors, how he finally found the village in Gambia from which his own ancestor had been captured and sold into slavery. This determination was made by a seventy-two-year-old village historian who was able to trace, in oral recitation covering 260 years and lasting many hours, the genealogy of one Kinte, from whom both he and Mr. Haley were descended.

Primitive societies honor the elderly, who are storehouses of knowledge. Rites and ceremonies that embody important ideas are made spectacular and emotional to impress the memory.

Primitive people believe in the power of the human voice— the magic of speech and song. The following, from the autobiography of a Papago woman as transcribed by the anthropologist Ruth Underhill, illustrates the impact of the spoken word:

"The men from all the villages met at Basket Cap Mountain and there my father made them speeches, sitting with his arms folded and talking low as great men do. Then they sang the war songs: 'Oh, bitter wind, keep blowing / That therewith my enemy / Staggering forward / Shall fall. . . .'

"Many, many songs they sang, but I, a woman, cannot tell

* Garden City, N.Y.: Doubleday, 1976.

120

you all. I know that they made the enemy blind and dizzy with their singing."*

However, as Harold Innis, the Canadian historian, wrote, "Richness of oral tradition made for a flexible civilization, but not one which could be disciplined to the point of effective political unity."** Primitive societies therefore were rarely large.

The written word brought into being a new social distinction, that between the literate and the illiterate, or peasant. The peasant is not simply an illiterate among illiterates, as in primitive societies, but one who is ruled by a literate ruling class of priests, seers, and magicians in the service of (as a rule) a military aristocracy. The high priests of ancient Egypt, like the mandarins of China and the ecclesiastics of medieval Europe, held a monopoly on the important secrets of the society, and the peasant could do nothing but obey his betters.

But literacy brought something much more important into being. Written words can be read and reread, thought about, compared and pondered. Statements can be examined for logical consistency. General agreement may be sought among many. Words might remain magical to the peasant, but to the priest and scholar they became instruments of coherent thought, of socially shared ideas and perceptions—and therefore of science.

Printing broke the knowledge monopoly of the priests and mandarins. In European history perhaps the most serious consequence of printing was the publication of translations of the Bible in vernacular languages—English, French, German. The work of people like Wycliffe and John Huss eventually broke the monopoly of Rome and led to the rise of one Protestant sect after another. This process continues to this day, because the central idea of Protestantism (if I may oversimplify vastly) is, "Read the Bible for yourself, and you will see the light," as compared with the Catholic teaching (also vastly oversimplified), "Listen to the priest, who will interpret the Bible for you."

"The book," says David Riesman of Harvard University, "helps

---

* David Riesman, "The Oral Tradition, the Written Word, and the Screech Image," in *Abundance for What?* Garden City, N.Y.: Doubleday, 1964, pp. 419–420.

** Harold A. Innis, *The Bias of Communication.* Toronto: University of Toronto Press, 1951, p. 10.

liberate the reader from his group and its emotions, and allows the contemplation of alternative responses and the trying on of new emotions. . . . The book tends to be a solvent of authority."*

Quite unlike the television program, the book can be enjoyed at one's own pace. It can be read and reread and reflected upon as it generates aspirations and dreams. Aspirations and dreams—like those of Benjamin Franklin, Abraham Lincoln, Thomas Edison, Emily Dickinson, Harry Truman—separate one from the crowd and ultimately create an individual, a unique human individual, and not "just one of the gang."

No wonder Andrew Carnegie believed that the best thing he could do for people was to build libraries. Indeed, I do not know how it is possible to become an individual in today's world without the private adventures of the mind provided by reading.

---

* Riesman, pp. 424–425.

Television and the Now Generation

A society is held together by great networks of communication which impose a certain degree of conformity on its members. These networks of communication may be rigidly demanding, as in Communist dictatorships, or they may be permissive, as in America. But even when the social control exercised by the networks is permissive, we are all deeply affected by them.

What are these networks? First there is the church, says David M. Potter of Stanford University, which "conceives of man as an immortal soul." It is the task of the church to tell us to be upright and honest and godly. It tells us to forgo the temptations and lusts of the present in the interests of a better life in the hereafter.

Another network of communication is education, which conceives of man, in Professor Potter's words, "as a being whose behavior is guided by reason. . . . The schools have made it their business to stimulate ability and to impart skills."* Hence schools and colleges tell us to make the most of our talents, to be rational, to be intelligent.

Business and industry are other networks of communication, which look upon human beings "as productive agents who can create goods or render services that are useful to mankind." So the world of business and industry says to us that we should work hard, invest wisely, increase productivity—and the free enterprise system will reward us for our efforts.

Although Potter does not list government as an instrument of social control—perhaps it is too obvious—it might well be

* David M. Potter, Chapter VIII, "The Institution of Abundance: Advertising," *People of Plenty.* Chicago: University of Chicago Press, 1954, pp. 168–188.

included. Government conceives of people as citizens, upon whose sense of civic responsibility the well-being of society rests. Be a good citizen, says government. Be loyal. Pay your taxes. Vote. Work for the good of your community and your nation.

Advertising too is an instrument of social control. It tells us what to eat, what to wear, how to do housework, what kind of car to drive. The correct nationally advertised brand will assure us, we are told, domestic bliss, sexual fulfillment, and the envy and respect of our neighbors. All human aspirations are translated by advertising into consumable merchandise.

As contrasted with other forms of social control, says Potter, "advertising has in its dynamics no motivation to seek the improvement of the individual or to impart qualities of social usefulness. . . . And though it wields an immense social influence, comparable to the influence of religion and learning, it has no social goals and no social responsibility for what it does with its influence. . . . It is this lack of institutional responsibility, this lack of inherent social purpose to balance social power, which, I would argue, is a basic cause for concern about the role of advertising."

These words were written thirty-five years ago in Professor Potter's book *People of Plenty,* but there is no reason to suppose that they are not even truer today. In those three decades the television commercial has come of age, so that advertising has become a more pervasive and penetrating influence in our lives than ever.

Since the basic purpose of advertising is to stimulate the desire to consume, it makes appeals to vanity ("Bring out the real you!"), to social emulation ("Isn't it time you had one too?"), to self-indulgence ("You owe it to yourself"). And always the urgent suggestion that you buy right away ("Hurry, hurry to your friendly Buick dealer!"), whether you have the money or not ("Small down payment, easy terms"). Never a word about waiting until you can afford it. Never a word about the years of study and training required to get the job to earn the necessary money. Buy now, while the impulse is upon you! Thus are the most powerful instruments of persuasion of all time directed toward the encouragement of impulse buying, of instant gratification.

Instant gratification is all right, I am sure, in a primitive culture in a warm climate—perhaps an island in the South Seas, where the lagoons are full of fish and coconuts fall at one's feet. But ever since man began to till the soil and learned not to eat the seed grain but to plant it and wait for the harvest, the postponement of gratification has been the basis of a higher standard of living and of civilization.

Perhaps there is an explanation of the hippie counterculture of the 1960s after all. Like South Sea Islanders, young people in America were brought up in the midst of abundance. They were also the first generation to have had television sets as baby-sitters—and they absorbed the message.

They are still with us. They are the Now Generation. They can't wait. Instant friendship. Instant love. Instant ecstasy. Instant satori. Wow!

Television as a Cause
of Social Revolution

The great and revolutionary communications instrument of the present in the United States is television. What it has done to the nation has not yet been measured, and what it will eventually do cannot now be predicted. A revolution in communications is always a far more important thing than is realized at the time. I wonder how many people have thought of the degree to which the revolution of rising expectations in Latin America, Asia, and Africa is due to the portable radio? In little villages all over Africa people who formerly had almost no cultural contacts beyond the next village gather today around portable, battery-operated radios to hear the news from London, New York, Paris, Tokyo, and Moscow—and therefore they start wanting to become citizens of a larger world than they have ever known before. Like radio, television bypasses literacy. Before the advent of radio and television, to be illiterate was to be cut off from the world. But now the illiterate, whether in Zaïre, in Mississippi, or in New York, can hear about and concern themselves with matters they formerly knew nothing about.

Television spread with greater rapidity among the poor than among the rich in the United States, among the uneducated than among the educated. Long before the upper middle class had made up their minds about the wisdom of buying a television set and exposing their children to it, forests of television antennae had risen above tenement homes in the depressed and slum districts throughout the country. In the socioeconomic pattern of the spread of television over America, blacks hold an important place. I recall from about 1951 a telephone call I received from an almost illiterate black drummer—a friend with whom I had worked many times in giving lecture-demonstrations on jazz history. He called to tell me that he was broke, out of a job, and willing to work at anything to make a little money, and he gave this touching picture of his poverty: "Me and my wife just moved into this apartment, Doc. We ain't got a stick of furniture, not even a bed. All we got is our television set."

Another important fact about television is that it is a much more expensive medium than radio. Radio is cheap enough so that small groups can organize and pay for programs and stations of their own—foreign-language groups, religious denominations, connoisseurs of classical music or traditional jazz, and the like. In almost every large city, therefore, for a decade and more there have been all-black radio stations featuring black talent, black news, black church services. Television is too expensive to be supported by any such minority, hence most television programs are addressed to the whole community. This means that whatever the television set says to white people, it also says to blacks.

But because of this strongly commercial basis of American television, there is a certain kind of Darwinian democracy in the programming. Commercial TV shows must appeal to the public. If viewers become bored, they switch channels, ratings go down, sponsors vanish, and the show is taken off the air. As a consequence, there exists a good deal of healthy competition among the stations and networks. They cannot simply impose their own private ideas on the public; they must discover what Americans want to see, then attempt to program those public desires in newscasts and historical dramas, soap operas and quiz shows, cartoons and Westerns.

Because of—not in spite of—its commercial nature, television reflects social values as well as causes them. The most immediate impression we may get from an average daily assortment of TV shows is one of astounding, almost dizzying variety—"rich mixed feeding," to use Huxley's phrase describing radio programming in the 1950s. But when we expand our knowledge of the extent of television's influence, we begin to see the true implications of its worldwide coverage and worldwide audience. Television becomes a cultural unifier, a "tribal drum of the global village."

Consider for a moment the world's image of the American West.

In Germany there are some sixty-three Western Clubs, societies whose members vacation in log cabins, dress up as cowboys and Indians, and even use saddles for pillows. Some hard-core members dress Western just to watch their favorite gunslinger episodes on television.

Italy has produced hundreds of "spaghetti Westerns," modeled on a compound of "Bonanza," Zane Grey, and Puccini's *Girl of the Golden West.*

Japan sports dozens of Western restaurants, features Japanese cowboy shows, and has recently started a *Frontier* magazine.

Levi's are so much in demand in the Soviet Union that they sell for a month's salary.

Now, one can take a scholar's point of view and point out how oversimplified, underplotted, or unrealistic these visions of the West must be. But the point is this: Television Westerns have informed the world's viewing population with the message: "Here is the American past, in all its violence, heroism, and abundance." What the non-American populaces think of us is, to a large extent, based upon this and other comparable social images transmitted by commercial television.

There are other factors which reinforce the effectiveness of TV as an instrument for social change. We go to school to improve our minds, to learn new things, out of a sense of duty to ourselves and what we would like our future to be. But television is something we watch for fun. Most people will, by all indications, watch TV all their lives, several hours a day. And so, even though the messages it transmits and the attitudes it assumes may not be as deep as those inherent in education, they are repeated more insistently.

"Send your son to school," someone once said, "and the boys there will educate him." But now, we let our children sit at the feet of ABC, CBS, and NBC. There is where the myths of our children are forming. There is the real source of television as an agent of social education. It is the most recent product of the Industrial Revolution applied to two of man's deepest needs: the hunger for information and the desire for entertainment. It is a revolution conducted not by bullets and pamphlets but by programming.

But if the television revolution eventually produces a universal passion for instant gratification, who will be left to do the hard work, the tedious chores, the laborious research and development needed to keep an abundant supply of consumer goods flowing?

PART VI
COMMUNICATION: INTERRACIAL AND INTERCULTURAL

"*Giri* to One's Name": Notes on the Wartime Relocation and the Japanese Character

Disaster followed upon disaster after the Japanese attack on Pearl Harbor. On that same day Japanese forces landed on the Malay Peninsula and began their drive toward Singapore. Guam fell on December 10, Wake on December 23. On December 8 Japanese planes destroyed half the aircraft on the airfields near Manila. As enemy troops closed in, General MacArthur withdrew his forces from the Philippines and retired to Australia. On Christmas Day the British surrendered Hong Kong.

The West Coast of the United States, rich with naval bases, shipyards, oil fields, and aircraft factories, seemed especially vulnerable to attack. There was talk of evacuating the entire Pacific Coast. How frightening were the nightly blackouts during that bleak winter of defeat! Would Japanese carriers come to bomb the cities? Would their submarines sneak through the Golden Gate to shell San Francisco? Would they actually mount an invasion? Who could tell?

War of course breeds fear of enemies within—spies, saboteurs. There were rumors that Japanese farmers in Hawaii had cut arrows in their fields to direct Japanese fighter pilots to Pearl Harbor, and that West Coast Japanese were equally organized to help the enemy. Such rumors were later found to be totally without foundation, but in the anxieties of the moment they were believed.

It was a field day for inflammatory journalists and newscasters: Westbrook Pegler, John B. Hughes—even Damon Runyon. The columnist Henry McLemore wrote, "Herd 'em up, pack 'em off and give 'em the inside room in the badlands. . . . Let us have no patience with the enemy or with any whose veins carry his blood. . . . Personally I hate the Japanese. That goes for all

131

of them." Walter Lippmann joined the cry for mass evacuation. Many felt that, in the event of invasion, it would be impossible to distinguish between the loyal and disloyal Japanese, and that therefore the prudent thing to do was to intern them all.

On February 19, 1942, President Roosevelt signed Executive Order 9066, which set in motion the evacuation program. It applied to all Japanese, citizens and noncitizens alike, in the three Western states and a portion of Arizona. Assembly centers were set up for them at fairgrounds and racetracks. From these they were transferred to ten semipermanent relocation camps in underpopulated, mostly desert areas, such as Minedoka, Idaho; Heart Mountain, Wyoming; Amache, Colorado; Rohwer, Arkansas; Manzanar, California (which had also been an assembly center).

Altogether some 110,000 were relocated, of whom more than 70,000 were American citizens by birth; the remainder were not able to become citizens under the laws then prevailing.

The relocation centers were dreary places: long rows of tarpaper-covered wooden barracks behind barbed wire, guarded by armed sentries. Each room had a stove, a drop light, an iron cot and mattress. Meals were served in large mess halls, meetings were held in bare recreation halls. But the War Relocation Authority (WRA), headed by the wise and humane Dillon Myer (a Midwesterner who before his appointment had known almost nothing about Japanese-Americans), encouraged camp self-government, hired teachers from outside to continue the education of the children, mediated quarrels among the internees, and made life as comfortable as possible for them.

The officials and staff of the WRA were, with few exceptions, deeply concerned about the injustice of the relocation program and eager to restore the Japanese-Americans, especially the Nisei (second generation), to normal American lives. They fanned out over the United States east of the Rockies to seek employment for the internees. As early as September 1942 hundreds of Issei (first generation) railroad workers were restored to their jobs in eastern Oregon. Thousands of Nisei went to Illinois, Minnesota, Ohio, New York, Alabama.

Everywhere the Japanese-Americans went, they impressed their employers by their industry and loyalty, so that more were summoned from the camps—scientists, teachers, mechanics, food processors, agricultural workers. By the time the order excluding the Japanese from the West Coast was rescinded on January 2, 1945, half the internees had found new jobs and homes in mid-America and the East.

It was a great humiliation for the Nisei of the 100th Battalion of the Hawaii National Guard to be sent to Camp McCoy, Wisconsin, where they were trained with wooden guns. Spark Matsunaga, now a U.S. Senator, who was in that unit, writes, "We wrote home of our great desire for combat duty to prove our loyalty to the United States. It was not known to us then that our letters were being censored by higher authority. We learned subsequently that because of the tenor of our letters, the War Department decided to give us our chance. Our guns were returned to us, and we were told that we were going to be prepared for combat duty. . . . Grown men leaped with joy."

On January 28, 1943, the War Department announced that Nisei would be accepted as a special combat unit. They volunteered in the thousands both from Hawaii and from the relocation camps. They were united with the 100th Battalion as the 442d Regimental Combat Team at Camp Shelby, Mississippi.

The 100th Battalion first saw action at Salerno, Italy, in September 1943, and took heavy casualties at Volturno, Cassino, and the Anzio beachhead. The 442d landed in Italy in June 1944, at once gained a reputation as an assault force, and in the Vosges Mountains in France accomplished the famous rescue of the "lost battalion" of the 36th (Texas) Division at an enormous cost in blood. Fighting in seven major campaigns, the men of the 442d suffered 9,486 casualties and won more than 18,000 individual decorations for valor.

Another 3,700 Nisei served in combat areas in the Pacific as translators and interpreters. The Japanese military, believing their language to be too difficult for foreigners to master, were careless about security. They did not count on Nisei on every battlefront reading captured documents and passing information on to Allied commanders. Kibei (Nisei born in America but educated in Japan and originally the object of special distrust) turned out to be especially helpful in this respect.

In short, the Nisei covered themselves with honor and made life in America better for themselves, their parents (who a few years after the war won the right to be naturalized), and their children. I remember vividly the returning Nisei veterans I saw in Chicago soon after V-E Day. Short of stature as they were, they walked proudly, infantry combat citations on their chests, conscious that they were home—in their own country. Chicago, known throughout the war for its hospitality to servicemen, out-did itself when the Nisei returned. They had earned that welcome.

The relocation was a heart-breaking experience for Japanese-Americans as well as a serious economic loss for those who had spent decades of labor on their farms and businesses. But most seriously it was an affront. America was saying to them, "You are not to be trusted. We doubt your loyalty."

The Nisei, although very much Americanized, are in some respects profoundly Japanese. An imputation of disloyalty, being an affront, was also a challenge. A powerful Japanese motivation is *"giri* to one's name"—the duty to keep one's reputation un-blemished. One accused of disloyalty is dutybound to remove that disgrace by demonstrating himself to be loyal beyond all expectation, so that the accuser must withdraw the charge with, "I'm sorry. I was wrong about you."

This is a basic reason the Nisei volunteered in such numbers and fought so well. More than 33,000 Nisei served in the war— a remarkable number out of a total Japanese-American popula-tion (Hawaii and mainland combined) of little more than 200,000. They had a fierce pride in their reputation as a group.

The Issei were also motivated by *"giri* to one's name." Those who found jobs outside the camps were exemplary workers, as if to prove something not only about themselves but about their entire group. Japanese-Americans, young and old alike, accepted the humiliation of mass relocation with dignity and maturity, making the best of an intolerable situation. In so doing they exhibited the finest resources of their ancient background cul-ture.

Many angry voices have been raised in recent years denounc-ing the "racism" of the relocation. To this I must say yes— and no. Yes, because California has had a history of anti-Oriental agitation since gold-mining days, and the other Western states for almost as long. Yes, because agricultural interests that have had to compete with Japanese farmers were quick to use racist slogans to drive them out and, where possible, seize their lands.

But much more important than racist sentiments against the Japanese was unfamiliarity with them. The main thrust of Japanese immigration had taken place between 1900 and 1925, when the Japanese Exclusion Act was passed. (The Chinese, who were more numerous, had begun arriving during the Gold Rush.) The average age of Nisei in 1941 was fifteen or sixteen. The average age of Issei—they had married late because they had had to make a place for themselves in America before sending for a bride—was fifty or over.

The average white American in 1941, even in the West, had therefore not known Japanese children as classmates, nor was he acquainted with the Issei, many of whom spoke English poorly or not at all and therefore kept to themselves.

Suddenly involved in a war with the Japanese, it became important to know what they were like and where their loyalties lay. It was widely reported, for instance, that reverence for the emperor was taught in the Japanese-language schools that many Nisei children attended after regular school. (This was true.) What was not known until after the war was that, despite this indoctrination, they had grown up loyal Americans.

It is sometimes asked why, if the relocation was not racist, Germans and Italians were not evacuated too. The answer is obvious. Germans and Italians, having come to America earlier than the Japanese and in far greater numbers, were already well-known to Americans in 1941. Besides, the West Coast feared an attack from Japan, not from Italy or Germany. The Japanese in Hawaii were not evacuated either, although there was some talk of shipping them all to Molokai, because to a far greater degree than on the mainland, they were known and trusted there. As well, their removal would have left Hawaii without an adequate labor supply even if there had been enough ships to remove them.

As one talks with Nisei today—they are now in their fifties and sixties—one gets the impression that the wartime relocation, despite the injustices and economic losses suffered, was perhaps the best thing that could have happened to the Japanese-Americans of the West Coast. As many say, the relocation forced them out of their segregated existence to discover the rest of America.

It opened up possibilities for them that they never would have known had they remained on farms in Livingston or fishing boats in San Pedro.

Urged by their high school teachers in the relocation centers or financed by the GI Bill, many Nisei who otherwise would never have gone to college went to Oberlin, Penn State, Wisconsin, Tulane, Illinois Tech, and elsewhere. A few remain bitter about the relocation, but most were too busy taking advantage of their new opportunities and pursuing their careers to nurse their grievances.

Determined to prove themselves in civilian life no less than in war, the Nisei have become a power in politics quite disproportionate to their numbers: three United States senators and, at present, two congressmen (there were three in the 94th Congress), plus numerous mayors and city officials. They hold influential positions in public school systems and in higher education. In business and agriculture they flourish like the green bay tree.

In his book *Race and Economics,** Thomas Sowell, a black economist who has studied the comparative progress of ethnic minorities in America, writes of the unintended benefits of the relocation program:

> One of the turning points in the evolution of Japanese-Americans was the partial undermining of family authority during their internment in World War II, and the subsequent release of many of the young Japanese-Americans from the camps to seek their individual fortunes throughout the country *without* parental guidance or authority. From their success, apparently the family had given them what they needed to succeed, except for greater individual freedom, which they now acquired as a by-product of unusual circumstances.

What did Japanese-Americans communicate that ultimately made them full citizens of the United States? Since their words would not have been believed, especially in wartime, they communicated by action and behavior. "We are good Americans," they said. "We are good neighbors. We are useful and productive citizens. We love America and are willing to die for her." These messages were communicated by the industry of workers and businessmen and farmers, by their service to the communities

* New York: David McKay, 1975.

in which they live, by their behavior as good citizens, and by the war record of the 442d. *It was a form of communication for which there is no verbal or symbolic substitute.*

The relocation thus resulted in the Americanization of the Japanese in one generation after immigration—a record for non-English-speaking immigrants of any color. This outcome was due in part to the nature of Japanese culture. In the face of rejection the Japanese do not blame those who reject them; if they want not to be rejected, they simply say, "The responsibility is our own." Their success is also due to the fact that America remains an open society, so that racism in America is neither as implacable nor as enduring as some would have us believe.

The Japanese-American Generation Gap

My Aunt Mary Satoe Furuyama died in her sleep at Woodlawn Hospital in Chicago in 1975 at the age of seventy-seven. She had had a rewarding life, full of family love and joy. She had also experienced hardships, including being put into a wartime relocation center at Rohwer, Arkansas, with her husband and children in 1942. I first became acquainted with the Furuyamas in 1945. Before that, I had not even known of their existence, since my father and Mary, although brother and sister, were far apart in age, had emigrated at different times, and had lost touch with each other.

Mrs. Furuyama's story is that of many Issei (first generation) immigrant Japanese women. She came to the United States as a picture bride in the period of the First World War. She settled in Modesto, where her husband, George, worked as a bartender in the Modesto Club. He was a man of some cultivation but few would have guessed it because of his atrocious English, which was just as bad as his wife's. The couple had three children—Bill, Helen, and Chuck. When the relocation of West Coast Japanese was ordered, the Furuyamas were running a small hotel in Stockton, where they had moved in 1929. Whatever business or property they had, they lost in the relocation.

The Furuyamas immediately began to look for ways to get out of their relocation camp. Bill had been drafted in 1942. He was given basic training several times over, while the army tried to figure out what to do with its Japanese-American recruits. While he was at Camp Grant, near Rockford, he made frequent trips to Chicago to look for a place for his family to live and to find out if they would be welcome there. Eventually, Bill served with the 442d and was wounded three times. Chuck, too young to get into the fighting, served with the United States occupation forces in Germany and Belgium.

The Furuyama family were among the first to get out of the relocation centers. Helen found a job in Chicago and helped find employment for her parents, so that they too could leave. Mary and George were in Chicago by 1945, working at the Edgewater Beach Hotel, she as a chambermaid, he as a maintenance man. She never complained about doing "menial work"; she found all work honorable and pleasurable. Perhaps the most important thing to be learned from Aunt Mary is that it is possible to endure hardship and injustice without rancor or bitterness. When I asked her once how she felt about the relocation, she replied, "What you expect? There was war."

Many years after the relocation centers had been closed, the United States government partially compensated the Japanese for their wartime losses of property. Aunt Mary got about $2,000, although she had lost much more than that. She did not complain. Having long since reconciled herself to the loss, she was overcome with gratitude at the American government's attempt to make amends. "They didn't need to do that," she said.

A few years ago she visited Japan, which she had not seen since she had been in her early twenties. When I visited our family home in Yamanashi some years later, I heard that Aunt Mary had boasted so much about America and was so proud of her American children that her Japanese relatives found her more than a little trying.

I am proud that Mary Furuyama was my aunt. She, like other Japanese immigrants of her generation, exhibited in her life the best qualities of her background culture—patience, industry, the ability to suffer misfortune without complaint, and the total absence of paranoia.

If the Japanese had been paranoiac about the injustices inflicted on them, as fashionable radicalism today urges all minorities to be, they would merely have reinforced the prejudices against them. But because they accepted with quiet dignity the insanities of a wartime climate of opinion, prejudice against them has all but disappeared, even in California, the original home of all the propaganda against the "Yellow Peril." The radical left, like the radical right, is unwilling or unable to understand that paranoia is a mental illness, not a program of social action.

A continuing controversy has filled the pages of Japanese-American publications for some years now. It was triggered by a book by Bill Hosokawa, of the *Denver Post,* entitled *Nisei: The Quiet Americans.** The image of the Japanese as quiet, conforming, and eager to adapt to the majority culture was vehemently rejected by some Japanese-Americans, especially the student radicals among the Sansei in the late 1960s. The Sansei, or third generation, the grandchildren of the Issei, as a rule do not speak, read, or write Japanese. The radicals among them declared proudly that they are not quiet, like the generation of their parents. They believed in loud protest against American imperialism and capitalism. As they tooled around in their Jaguars and Corvettes, they cried, "Down with the white power structure!" Believing themselves to be racially oppressed, they called each other "brother" and "sister" and shouted "Right on!" in fashionable imitation of radical blacks.

Naturally, all this had led to a lot of self-examination and soul searching and finger-pointing in the Japanese-American press. The Riverside, California, chapter of the Japanese-American Citizens League, in an interesting statement on some of these matters, argued that Japanese-Americans have assimilated quickly into the mainstream culture because there are large areas of similarity between the values and goals of the Japanese and American cultures.

"Both Japanese and white middle-class culture," writes Hosokawa, "share in common the values of politeness, respect for authority and parental wishes, duty to community, diligence, cleanliness and neatness, emphasis on personal achievement of long-range goals . . . the importance of keeping up appearances. The virtues of persistence, determination in the face of—even impossible—odds are warrior (Samurai) virtues inculcated into all Japanese youth. These virtues, whether exhibited as soldiers, students, or employees, won the respect of Americans. Thus by being most Japanese, the Nisei became the most readily Americanized."

If the Riverside chapter and Bill Hosokawa are correct in their explanation of the success of Japanese-American assimilation,

* New York: William Morrow, 1969.

the Sansei who tried to seek their ethnic identity by emulating the radical postures of their white and black college peers were caught in a dilemma. The more they rejected quietness, conformity, discipline, and the "stereotype" of the well-behaved Japanese in the mistaken belief that such traits are "the result of submission to white racist oppression," the farther they got from their cultural roots. It is not Japanese, but American, as the Riverside chapter points out, to assert the primacy and independence of the individual.

I am not unsympathetic to the young person trying to find out, as the grandchild of immigrants, "who he is." Nor do I deny that discrimination can make a person feel less than a whole human being. However, I deplore the present fashion of magnifying discrimination against Japanese-Americans as a way of getting into the act. The Japanese in America are not being discriminated against in any economic, or even social, way today. In California they have a higher level of income and education than the average of the population. Nowadays more than fifty percent of marriages of persons with Japanese surnames are with people of non-Japanese, non-Oriental surname.

As for myself, I have been accused by Sansei radicals in the Japanese-American press as "never having shared the Nisei experience." Somehow, I always thought that, being a Nisei myself, whatever happened to me was a Nisei experience, including election to the U.S. Senate. Nisei are not all alike, in spite of the silly stereotypes of the radicals' new racism. Some Nisei occupy high political positions; others are apolitical. Some are scientists; others are hippies. A few Nisei are millionaires; a few are very poor. Some are pillars of their local chamber of commerce; others are mystics. We all contribute a portion of the definition of what it is to have belonged to our generation. America, too, is a generalization made up of a vast number of individual experiences. The "melting pot" today is much maligned, but I think it is not understood. It is not so much the acceptance of conformity; it is rather that each American, knowing that the amalgam from the melting pot will be a little bit different because it has included him and his difference, can feel that the American future remains exciting, unpredictable—and something to dazzle the world.

Racial Pride vs. Racial Obsession

The philosophy of determinism says that people are the product of outside forces. The delinquent becomes so because of a broken home. The criminal becomes so because he was brought up in a slum. The poor are poor because society never gave them a chance. The motto of determinism is, "It isn't their fault." When determinism is applied to one's self, it becomes, "It isn't my fault."

For blacks the determinist explanation of their condition has obvious attractions. We are uneducated, they may say, because white school boards give us inferior schools. We are poor because both employers and unions discriminate against us. We who are in prison are not really criminals, but "political prisoners." According to this view, there is no black problem. There is just one huge white problem, which will continue until whites cure themselves of their racism.

Orlando Patterson, professor of sociology at Harvard, who is himself black, writing on "The Moral Crisis of Black Americans" in the summer 1973 issue of *The Public Interest,** said that determinism "is totally unacceptable as the ethical basis of black moral life." The question is not whether the black American's present condition is the result of white oppression, past and present, since it largely is. The question is what to do with this fact.

If one concludes that his failure in life "is entirely the consequence of another group . . . it follows that only that group can change one's conditions. The oppressed become totally the

* Pp. 43–69.

product and creature of the oppressor. . . . Morally, this is a pathetic condition."

Patterson continues, "The victim who cries, 'Help me! You have crippled me; now make me whole again,' is simply contemptible. . . . There can be no moral equality where there is a dependency relationship among men." Hence there is no moral difference between the humble pleader for help and the militant with his nonnegotiable demands. "He may cry with cap in hand or holler; that is to say, eeny-meeny, a Booker T. Washington, or miny-mo, an Eldridge Cleaver. Both are in the morally humiliating position of saying, 'Our fate is in the white man's hands.' "

With the determinist framework, the black leader can exploit white guilt. To cry, "We have been wronged!" is a strategy that pays off handsomely—but only at the cost of one's moral dignity. Hence, Patterson believes, the black man must "move from the vicious grip of determinism into the personal dignity and freedom of a morally autonomous view of the world."

How can the black man achieve the moral transformation to assume total responsibility for himself and his community? First, says Patterson, he must not look to the white man for help. The responsibility is the black man's alone. Ultimately the moral transformation must come from a refusal to remain caught in the determinist trap.

Patterson discerns three forms of this refusal, which he calls "rebellion." It begins with the assertion, "I am responsible for myself." One form of the rebellion against determinism is "usurpation," in which the oppressed "take over the culture and life style of the oppressor. After all, what better role-model of an autonomous group is there than that of a ruling elite?" Like the "English Cockney who goes the well-trodden ascending route of Grammar School, Oxford and the Labour aristocracy," American blacks can rise to positions of influence and power, achieving fulfillment for both themselves and their race. There is, of course, the danger of selling out in the course of one's rise. But, says Patterson, "black history is replete with black cultural usurpers who have been strong defenders of and workers for their race"—for example, W. E. B. DuBois and Frederick Douglass.

Spiritual withdrawal is another kind of rebellion against determinism. It is the retreat from social injustice into fundamentalist Christianity, which, "by placing the blame for sin and failure squarely on the individual . . . presents Blacks with an autonomous oasis of dignity and personal worth." In confirmation of Patterson's views, I would mention the Negro church members of my acquaintance, most of whom refuse to be called blacks. They have a high sense of self-worth and personal moral responsibility, regardless of the level of their education or wealth. Many work uncomplainingly at menial jobs, supporting disabled husbands or aged parents, too proud to go on welfare.

The third kind of rebellion against determinism Patterson calls "existential," since it is an assertion of identity: "I rebel, therefore I exist." Thousands of black men and women, "coming from environments with the same sorry list of broken homes, crime-plagued neighborhoods, drug-infested streets, inadequate schools . . . nonetheless succeed. How are we to explain them? We cannot. They defy explanation precisely because they alone account for their success. They are, it seems to me, manifestations of the unpredictable human spirit, which determinists have never been able to account for.

"The same black person who declares himself proud and free," says Patterson, "might be seen going to cash a welfare check." Those who take any one of the paths Patterson describes are truly proud, truly free.

I remember a party of graduate students to which I was invited at the University of Chicago many years ago. The young people had just received their degrees and were celebrating. A pretty blond girl from Alabama, having just got her M.A. in anthropology, was especially radiant, her graduation being a symbol to her of her intellectual liberation from the prejudices of the Southern town in which she had been brought up.

But a black sociologist kept bugging her. "What would they think of you in Alabama if they knew you were at an interracial party?" he would ask. "Forget it, Joe," she would say. "We're in Chicago." However, Joe would persist, "What would your parents say if they saw you sitting on a sofa having drinks with a black man?" Finally the host had to intervene with, "Lay off it, Joe. Can't you think about anything but race?" But the trouble was that Joe couldn't.

Just as there are blacks who can't think about anything but their blackness, there are Jews who can't think about anything but their Jewishness. The world is full of people obsessed by their nationality or race.

I use the term "obsessed" to convey a distinction. It is one thing to be proud to be black or Jewish or whatever. Pride is based on love of fellow members of one's group. But obsession is a different emotion. It is often disguised as love, but it is actually based on fear and hate. The obsessed Jew is one who fears and hates gentiles. The obsessed black is one who hates whites. The obsessed white, like the Ku Klux Klansman, does not love his fellow whites nearly as much as he hates blacks.

There are no problems between Irish Catholics and Irish Protestants that cannot be solved with reason and goodwill. But Irish Catholics obsessed with their hatred of the British, and British-oriented Irish Protestants obsessed, like the Reverend Ian Paisley, with their hatred of Catholics, have neither reason nor goodwill. They will continue fighting each other until the end of time.

Blacks had reason to fear and hate whites after more than three hundred years of slavery, exploitation, and second-class citizenship in the United States. However, to speak only of recent times, men of law like Thurgood Marshall and men of religion like Martin Luther King, Jr., taught people fighting for their civil rights how to contain their fear and hatred and how to advance their cause by appeals to the best in human reason and human nature. No one can say their tactics were fruitless. Enormous strides toward legal justice, educational equality, and the advancement of economic opportunity were made in the 1950s and '60s—at a rate of advancement without precedent in American history.

But also in the '60s there was a new development. With the rise, thanks to television, of dramatic "instant leaders" like Stokely Carmichael, Rap Brown, Huey Newton, and Eldridge Cleaver, and above all with the tragic assassination of Dr. King, the civil rights climate changed dramatically. The new militants did not believe in trying to control their fear or hatred. Instead they moved from racial pride to racial obsession—perhaps because they didn't have enough pride to begin with. The power of law, so ably demonstrated by Thurgood Marshall, and the power of moral example, exemplified by Dr. King, were held up to scorn in favor of a belief in "the power that flows from the barrel of a gun."

The relations between white and black in America are complex beyond description. They are a mixture of trust and distrust, of love and murder, of exploitation and rebellion, of con games played on each other over the centuries, of cultural interpenetration, and ultimately of mutual dependency. Like a long-married but quarreling couple, they can neither get along with each other or without each other. Nevertheless, in a curious reversal of the flow of cultural influence, many black intellectuals and opportunistic black politicians have accepted the crude oversimplifications of street-gang thinking and welded them into an ideology. To hear some of them talk, all the problems of America, if not of the world, are due to malicious, imperialist, racist whites oppressing brave, long-suffering, savagely mistreated blacks. This is paranoia, pure and simple.

It all goes to show again that when Christ taught us to love and not to hate, He was not just teaching morality. He was teaching sanity.

Talking Oneself into Trouble

Since speakers and commentators refer so frequently nowadays to "self-fulfilling prophecies," I'd like to explain this important idea. A self-fulfilling prophecy is a statement that is neither true nor false, but is capable of becoming true if it is believed.

Suppose a teacher says of her class, "These children are not educable." If she believes what she says, she will approach her teaching tasks with low expectations and lower morale. She will treat her pupils as stupid—and they will respond by being sullen and unresponsive. And she will say, "What did I tell you?"

Suppose on the other hand, the teacher says, "This class is educable. They are culturally disadvantaged but I am sure they have intellectual potential." Then she will tackle her job with enthusiasm and energy. She will blame any failures she may experience on herself. She will try one approach after another until she begins to get results. And when she does, she will cry triumphantly, "What did I tell you?"

Long ago I knew in Chicago a black jazz musician with an uneven employment record and a drinking problem. Once when he was unemployed he called me for help. I referred him to a bookseller, who promptly gave him a stockroom job. Three or four days later the bookseller gave my friend several hundred dollars in cash to take to the bank for deposit. It was a new experience for my friend; he had never before worked for anyone who had shown any trust in him.

From that day onward my friend became a dependable employee. No matter how late he played a gig the night before, he was on time in the morning to open the shop and do his work. The employer's implicit statement, "This man can be trusted," proved to be a self-fulfilling prophecy.

We hear from all sides these days—from angry blacks as well as guilt-stricken whites—that "America is a racist society." What kind of statement is this? Is it a statement of verifiable fact, like "The Mississippi River flows into the Gulf of Mexico"? Is it an overgeneralization, attributing "racism" to all of American society when it can justly be attributed only to parts of it?

What I am afraid of is that the statement, reiterated often enough, may operate as a self-fulfilling prophecy. The young black man may say to himself, "Yes, this is a racist society. Let's not be deceived by the appearance of progress because a few Uncle Toms are being bought off with prominent jobs. The white ruling class will never relinquish its power and privileges. A black man really hasn't a chance, until he understands that power comes only from the barrel of a gun." Such a young man, believing that his only hope of self-realization must lie in violent counterattack, will join in attempts to "destroy the white power structure." If he continues in this path, he will really fulfill his own prophecy. As he lies dying of police-inflicted gunshot wounds, he will say, "What did I tell you!" He will never suspect the degree to which he brought his fate upon himself.

The world is in large part a world of hard fact. The Mississippi River does flow into the Gulf of Mexico, and won't flow into the Pacific Ocean no matter how eloquently anyone argues. But another part of the world—the world of social interaction—is the world of evaluations: "These children are uneducable"; "War with Russia is inevitable"; "America is a racist society." These are evaluations. Because they are evaluations they can become true if people believe them and act on their beliefs. They can be dissipated as mythology if people refuse to believe them and act on different assumptions: "These children can be educated"; "We can resolve our differences with the Soviet Union"; "The racial situation in America can improve or deteriorate, depending on how I choose to act."

A. E. Housman said, "I, a stranger and afraid, in a world I never made." Alfred Korzybski's comment on this line: "Don't be afraid. With your evaluations you made that world. With different evaluations you can make another one."

PART VII
THE LANGUAGE OF
SOCIAL AGREEMENT

The Language of Social Agreement

At some time around the age of three or four, children learn to react meaningfully to expressions like "It's my turn . . . it's Billy's turn next." "My turn" is something that cannot be pointed to; its meaning is not "referential" in the strictly positivist sense, nor is it merely "lyrical." Nevertheless, the meaning of the expression does lie within the nervous systems of the speaker and hearer. It is an elementary form of social agreement. It says something about both the present and the future. With the child's achievement of the ability to react meaningfully to "my turn" and "Billy's turn," there is rejoicing in the heart of his parent or play-school teacher, for the child has taken a significant step toward being socialized—which is to say, human.

The language of law is the most formidable and most formalized portion of that larger collection of linguistic events I call the language of social agreement. But in the very act of saying "language of social agreement," we distort the facts, since without the language there could not be the kind of social agreement that exists at the human level. The difference between use and ownership, between cohabitation and marriage, between a killing and a murder, is a linguistic product. "Cohabitation" says something about the present and perhaps, too, about the past; but it makes no commitments about the future. The very fact that commitments can be made rests upon our ability to talk—our ability to make abstractions and symbolizations about the future. "Sirloin next Sunday" is meaningless to a dog, since to a dog a sign has no significance unless its referent is present or immediately forthcoming. When human beings formulate goals for "next Sunday," for "thirty days after date," or "until death do us part," they thereby impose some kind of order and predictability upon behavior. Social agreements, which are commitments about the future, statements of intent, are made in language or they are not made at all. As Aldous Huxley writes:

> The existence of language permits human beings to behave with a degree of purposefulness, perseverance, and consistency unknown among the other mammals and comparable only to the purposefulness, perseverance and consistency of insects acting under the compulsive force of instinct. Every instant in the life, say, of a cat or a monkey tends to be irrelevant to every other instinct. Such creatures are the victims of their moods. Each impulse as it makes itself felt carries the animal away completely. Thus, the urge to fight will suddenly be interrupted by the urge to eat; the all absorbing passion of love will be displaced in the twinkling of an eye by a no less absorbing passion to search for fleas. The consistency of human behavior, such as it is, is due entirely to the fact that men have formulated their desires, and subsequently rationalized them, in terms of words. . . . If it were not for the descriptive and justificatory words with which we bind our days together, we should live like the animals in a series of discrete and separate spurts in impulse.*

Law is the mighty collective effort made by human beings to inhibit the "discrete and separate spurts of impulse" and to organize in their place that degree of order, uniformity, and predictability of behavior that makes society possible.

There is a tremendous difference, therefore, between the "predictability" of science and that of law. What science predicts ("Ice will melt at temperatures above 32° F") comes true independent of our volition. What law predicts ("Persons convicted of murder will be hanged") becomes true because we are resolved to do what we said we could do. At the basis of law is our own resolve—our "agreements," our "willingness," our "intent."

As Alfred Korzybski said, "Human beings are a symbolic class of life." Among the many things we do with our symbols is to organize not only our past experiences and our present perceptions, but also our future behavior. Language is not only descriptive, in the sense of supplying verbal maps of nonverbal territories, it is also prescriptive or directive in the sense of supplying

---

* *Words and Their Meanings.* Los Angeles: Jake Zeitlin, 1940, pp. 13–14.

us with verbal blueprints of nonverbal territories that we intend, through our own efforts, to bring into being. The language of law is of necessity, therefore, to a large degree hortatory. In addition to prescribing certain forms of behavior, it must also create the intent, the resolve, to follow prescription. The judge is to a large degree a preacher. The trial is a morality play.

Hortatory utterances are almost invariably stated at a higher level of abstraction and with a greater degree of dogmatism than the immediate situation calls for. The reasons for this are partly rhetorical: to get attention and to impress the directive firmly on the hearer's mind. The rhetoric in turn is dictated by the human need, of both the speaker and the hearer, for apparent "purposefulness, perseverance, and consistency" in human behavior.

To reduce this matter to a simple example, let us suppose that the purpose of a given hortative utterance is to get Junior to eat his peas. If the simple demand, "Junior, eat your peas," does not work, one proceeds immediately to a higher level of abstraction, "Vegetables are good for you," and "All growing boys should eat plenty of vegetables." In other words, my demand that Junior eat his peas is asserted to be not merely a passing whim, but the particularization of a general nutritive principle. If Junior still leaves his peas untouched, one appeals to history: "Your grandfather was a vegetarian, and he lived to the age of ninety-nine," and "Sailors in the old sailing ships used to die of scurvy because they didn't get enough fresh vegetables." From here on, it is but a short jump to say that God intended that peas be eaten and that fathers be obeyed.

But the great principles we enunciate on one day prove to be extremely inconvenient on another day, as inevitably they must, since they stated so much more than was necessary to begin with. So as Father himself leaves untouched the carrot-and-raisin salad a few days later, he can say if challenged, "What I was arguing for all along is not vegetables as such, but for a balanced diet—and it is possible to achieve balance without this particular salad. A man can't keep going on rabbit food. Did you know that Vilhjalmur Stefansson proved that one can live healthily and well on an all-meat diet? Do you know of the millions in Asia that are suffering from protein deficiency because they get nothing but vegetables to eat?" Thus do fathers keep all bases covered and strive to maintain the fiction of infallible wisdom.

If the layman regards the law with a mixture of exaggerated respect and exaggerated distrust, is it not because lawyers and judges perform in a spectacular and awe-inspiring way what the rest of us do daily? Judges, when they change the interpretation of the Constitution, are almost always at considerable pains to assert that their new interpretation is what the Constitution really meant all along. If we, as laymen, approve of the change, we agree that this is indeed what the Constitution meant all along; if we disapprove the change, we are aghast at the temerity of judges who take it upon themselves to "change the Constitution."

The hortatory habit of mind, if too uncritically indulged whether by laymen or by jurists, results in a proclivity for claiming for one's exhortations a longer-lasting validity and a wider generality of applicability than any immediate situation would warrant.

Breaking Up the Deadlock

Whenever we see a situation that is psychologically threatening, we tend to become rigid in our attitudes. Mr. A, the manager, says to Mr. B, the assistant manager, "I'd like you to do XYZ." Mr. B, finding the suggestion threatening for whatever reason, instead of saying, "Yes, sir" or "What exactly do you have in mind?" says, "Oh, yeah?"

Let us suppose that Mr. A finds that "Oh, yeah?" threatening. "Doesn't he recognize my authority?" he thinks to himself. "Can't he at least be civil?" Mr. A, if he is like many of us facing a problem of communication, may decide to say the same thing over again, only louder. This may be called communication by decibel.

Of course Mr. B doesn't like being shouted at. So his resistance increases, which of course Mr. A finds additionally threatening, so that he too becomes even more rigid.

What next? Another solution that occurs to Mr. A is "to say it in words of one syllable" so that Mr. B cannot fail to understand. Mr. B, who has only finished high school, while Mr. A has been to college, now finds that he is being talked down to—and becomes angry. In no time at all, two individuals are both highly threatened by the other and a complete communicative deadlock results.

Communicative deadlock is disastrous, but, in a way, fascinating. Sometimes it is a noisy situation, with two persons yelling at one another. Sometimes it is very quiet, because the two have stopped speaking to each other. Either way, what characterizes communicative deadlock is that, while messages may be being sent, none is being received.

The interminable truce negotiation at Panmunjom at the close

155

of the Korean War is a classic example of communicative dead-lock. The United Nations negotiators and the North Korean negotiators were equally threatened by each other, so that each side was rigidly locked inside its own defense. How can communicative deadlock be resolved? It certainly is not easy—neither in international relations nor in person-to-person encounters.

What Mr. A can do, if he finds he cannot get his message across, is actively to invite messages from Mr. B. This is obviously going to be hard to do, because he is already threatened by Mr. B, but if Mr. A is determined to reestablish communication, he has to take his courage in hand and do it: "Well, Mr. B, I take it that you don't think much of my suggestion. I wish you would tell me your objections."

Mr. B, still angry and defensive, will probably respond by saying, "Of course I object to it. It's simply a damn fool idea." Most of us, when we are angry or upset, are prone to use evaluative words like "silly," "nonsensical," "idiotic," and the like. If Mr. A reacts to these words with anger, the deadlock is on again. But let's assume Mr. A has some self-discipline and is determined to break through. He may say, "Yes, I know you think it's a foolish idea. But I wish you'd explain your objections to it." If Mr. A is patient enough, Mr. B will gradually find his defenses relaxing. Being invited to talk, he will begin to ask questions. Instead of evaluative expressions like "idiotic plan," he may say something like, "Isn't that the same plan we tried in Kansas City in 1971 that didn't work out?" This is a request for information, not simply an evaluation.

From here on Mr. A can say, "Oh, that's why you object to the plan. You see this as similar to what we tried in Kansas City?" Mr. B says, "Well, isn't it?" At this point, Mr. A may be tempted to argue, but he must hold himself in check and continue to invite the flow of Mr. B's ideas. "What else do you see wrong with the plan?" Because Mr. B's statements are becoming more factual than evaluative, Mr. A's defenses also relax. And Mr. B, having been generously listened to, may eventually say, "What exactly did you have in mind, suggesting XYZ?" So now Mr. A has a chance to explain.

If the communication between the two is successful, changes take place in both Mr. A and Mr. B. Each has learned something from the other. We might designate the change by calling them no longer A and B, but Mr. A-plus and Mr. B-plus. When A and B are not in communication with each other, they often find a problem insoluble. But they can solve it if, through mutual communication, they *become* A-plus and B-plus.

They will not solve it by compromise, but by arriving at a higher level of information about the problem, after which the solution becomes clear to both.

The new solution is neither A's nor B's. It is the product of the interaction between A-plus and B-plus. And that is what communication is for.

Politics: Never Satisfactory, Always Necessary

The language scholar Benjamin Lee Whorf (1897–1941) once said, "Whenever agreement or assent is reached in human affairs, this agreement is reached by linguistic processes, or else it is not reached."* By linguistic processes he meant, of course, discussion, argument, persuasion; definitions and judgments; promises and contracts—all those exchanges of words by means of which human beings interact with each other.

Without language—without words—there is no such thing as the future. "Mary and John are married" is a statement about the present and also the future; it points to the obligations that Mary and John have toward each other in the days and years ahead. The future is real to us because it is formulated into words. Society is a network of agreements about future conduct. Here, let us say, are two tribes, the Blues and the Reds. Both tribes want exclusive access to the fish in Clearwater Bay. If the two tribes are equally strong, they will fight and fight and kill each other—until someone has the good sense to say, "Since we can't lick them and they can't lick us, let's call a conference and see what we can work out."

What Benjamin Lee Whorf calls linguistic processes are initiated. Delegates from the two tribes argue and shout and scream, but ultimately they come to an agreement. The Reds will fish the bay Mondays, Wednesdays, and Fridays; the Blues on Tuesdays, Thursdays, and Saturdays; no fishing on Sundays.

People who work out agreements of this kind are known as politicians. Politicians are people who resolve through linguistic

* "Science and Linguistics," *The Technology Review*, April 1940, in S. I. Hayakawa, *Language in Action*. New York: Harcourt, Brace, 1941, pp. 302–321.

processes conflicts that would otherwise have to be solved by force. But politicians are rarely thanked for their efforts. Many of the Blues are disappointed. "Look at what the politicians gave away to the Reds," they say. "What a sellout! They must have been bribed." The Reds are equally critical of their delegates. "Everyone knows," they say, "that God intended the bay for the exclusive use of us Reds, but now the Blues act as if they had equal rights to it. What we need are delegates who are men of principle, not compromisers."

The results of a political process are never satisfactory to all concerned. Give the Arabs what they want, and the Israelis are enraged. Give the employers what they want, and the unions are furious. Introduce a measure of gun control, and the National Rifle Association is apoplectic. If the political process is successful, all get only part of what they want, and none gets all he wants. And everyone blames the politicians for their disappointments. It often seems that the political process is far too subtle, far too complex, for men of words—intellectuals and journalists—to understand. Intellectuals, with their passion for logic and order, often disdain the democratic process. They are fascinated by Plato's perfect republic governed by philosopher kings. Imagining themselves to be the "gold" of Plato's classification of human beings, intellectuals are easily seduced by Marxism, which insists that government should be in the hands of those who understand such arcane matters as dialectical materialism and historic necessity—that is, intellectuals. This is no doubt the reason that there are more Marxists than Democrats and Republicans combined in so many university departments of philosophy.

Mike Royko of the Chicago *Daily News,* a characteristic journalistic critic of politics, wrote a book entitled *Boss,** which attacked and criticized the late Mayor Richard Daley of Chicago as corrupt, venal, ruthless, and given to making shady alliances with the underworld and ridiculous mistakes in English grammar. The book has become quite a favorite in college courses in political science as required and recommended reading.

However, not long after the publication of Royko's book, Richard Daley was returned to office as mayor of Chicago, at the

* New York: E. P. Dutton, 1971.

age of seventy-three and no longer in the best of health, with the biggest majority of his long political career. Apparently there is something about politics that neither Mr. Royko nor political science teachers quite understand—and that is how successful practitioners of the art of politics like Mayor Daley earn the trust and affection of so many people.

Disgusted with politicians, people from time to time yearn for government without politics. Sometimes, to their dismay, they get it, as in Soviet Russia, China, Poland, and North Korea, where the political process has been abolished, or as in Northern Ireland, where the political process has failed.

As Americans we need more than ever today to understand and cherish the political process. It is admittedly untidy. It is confusing. But it is the very essence of civilization.

much—but let's not, for goodness' sake, go up to four point two. First, CETA has not proved itself to be an effective program for training people and getting them into jobs." And I expanded on this idea.

What, I said, does 7.4 percent unemployment mean? The percentage of adults working—65 percent—was the same in 1954 as it is in 1977, even though the unemployment figure was 5 percent in 1954 and 7.4 percent in 1977. The argument I gave was this: Unemployment in 1977 is not the same as unemployment in 1954.

In 1954 almost all those registered as unemployed were primary wage earners for their families. If they were unemployed, then the whole family was in distress. Today, with more and more women entering the job market, even if the primary wage earner (let's say the husband) is employed, the wife, or secondary wage earner, is likely to *register* as unemployed.

Secondary wage earners do not have as urgent a need for a job as primary wage earners. Furthermore, secondary wage earners do not have the intense job attachment of primary wage earners. They are more likely to quit if they are unhappy. Also, in the years since 1954 we have significantly increased the benefits and relaxed the conditions for employment insurance. So now, if you are bored with your job, you can leave, get the boss to agree that you were laid off, and collect the benefits.

The attractions of being officially unemployed have intensified hugely over the past twenty years. A friend of mine works for the Forest Service as a firefighter—a job in which he is needed only eight months of the year. He is laid off for the other four months, but gets unemployment benefits. What would he have done in 1954? He would have made his pay for eight months stretch out over twelve. But people rarely do that anymore. It is better to be registered as unemployed.

Thus there has been an enormous increase in voluntary unemployment. Secondary wage earners and people collecting unemployment benefits can be fussy about what jobs they take. Because they are not facing eviction or starvation, they can remain unemployed longer. The phenomenon that economists call structural unemployment is built into the economy and is not diminished by rising levels of prosperity. Indeed, if you have a rising level of prosperity you get more of that kind of unemployment, because people can quit their jobs, enjoy a paid vacation on their unemployment benefits, and remain confident that they can get jobs again when their benefits run out.

So the components that go into unemployment statistics in 1954 and in 1977 are different—if not entirely different, certainly different enough for us to be wary of comparisons. Faced with figures like 7.4 percent or 8 percent unemployment rates, people too often react with unjustified alarm. Isn't it a terrible situation, they say. We've got to appropriate billions to create jobs for all those people.

Such was the solution for unemployment in Roosevelt's day, and I believed in it then. But the solutions of 1935 are not entirely relevant to the economic situation in 1978. This is the point I wanted to make, as I argued against the jump from 2.2 to 4.2 for CETA. Not only did I introduce an amendment opposing the increase; I gave a twenty-five-minute speech about it. People got up to argue against me, so I argued right back, acting like an experienced senator.

The amendment was defeated by a vote of 60–29. I was very proud of those twenty-nine votes. You don't win them all. In the beginning, you don't even win one. The fact that I was defeated didn't matter a damn in a way. I was elated that I had got into the action. But my defeat matters to the taxpayer— two billion dollars' worth.

Sharing the wealth

The New Deal effected a great many changes in Americans' attitudes toward their government. I do not quarrel about its necessity at the time. But I'd like to discuss its consequences and to ask the question, What is government for?

For a long time, the function of government has been to maintain national security, to preserve domestic order and tranquillity, to regulate trade, and to write and administer the laws. At no time did the people of the United States amend the Constitution to say that another function of government is to redistribute income.

That, however, is the principal function of government today. Roy Ash, former director of the Office of Management and Budget, has pointed out that transfer payments—payments for aid to families with dependent children, food stamps, Medicaid, housing subsidies, supplementary Social Security income pro-

function of business in the world. I recall a long conversation with my father just before the beginning of World War II. He was then a prosperous importer and exporter in Osaka, doing business with Africa, Europe, Central America, the Dutch East Indies, and I don't know how many other places.

I visited Japan in 1935. At that time I was a brand-new Ph.D. in English from the University of Wisconsin, with a cultivated distaste for the materialistic businessman and his concern for profits. I asked my father what he exported, and to whom. I was aware that in those days "Made in Japan" was a synonym for junk merchandise. (This was before the days of Toyota, Sony, Nikon, Honda, and Kawasaki.)

Father said that, among other things, the company was at this time exporting imitation patent-leather shoes to Central America. At that point my scorn for his trade in junk must have been obvious, because he delivered a lecture to me that I have never forgotten.

He said, "Do you know what happens to those imitation patent-leather shoes when they are bought by a poor man in Central America?" I admitted I had no idea. "In the first place," he said, "if they were real leather, the poor man would not be able to afford them. When he goes to the city with them, he ties the laces together and hangs them around his neck and walks to town in sandals or barefoot.

"Then when he reaches the marketplace he puts them on. As he struts around in them, he examines glassware from Germany, silk scarves from Hong Kong, chocolates from Switzerland, canned peas and goose liver from France. All this gives him an intimation of a larger world than that of his little country village—and his outlook changes.

"He wants to belong to that larger world. If he can't do so himself, he dreams that possibly his children may. So he wants them to learn to read and write, so that they can belong to that larger world. And the moment that peasant, that illiterate peasant, says to himself, 'We don't have to be peons forever,' social change is on its way. And I am contributing to that social change with those imitation patent-leather shoes."

Years later, when students at San Francisco State College and elsewhere were shouting, "We are revolutionaries! We're going to overthrow the Establishment! We'll change the world! We're against anybody who stands in the way of social change!" I began to think about my father. I asked myself: What kind of people are the most subversive? From whom is there the most to fear in the way of social change? If you say the people to fear are Socialists, Communists, anarchists, I think you are wrong. The most subversive people in the world, I think, are businessmen.

A revolution, to be a revolution in any true sense, must change the relationship of social classes to one another. The United States is a profit-oriented industrial society. Because the United States is capable of the mass production of consumer goods, it has mass consumption—and advertising to stimulate that consumption. The unintended revolution created by mass production and mass consumption has come close to producing a classless society in America. Executives and workingmen alike drive Comets and Cadillacs, drink Coke and Schlitz and Old Grand-Dad, eat Nabisco wafers and Hormel ham, and watch the Johnny Carson show.

There is no "ruling class." Anyone can become President, including a graduate of Harvard (John F. Kennedy), of Southwest State Teachers College (Lyndon B. Johnson), of Whittier College (Richard M. Nixon), or of no college at all (Harry S. Truman)—and, after attaining that lofty height, he can still be impeached.

And the poor of America are not poor by world standards. Our welfare clients live far better than the working people of more than half the world.

We are people of plenty. We have become so through our energy, our inventiveness, our encouragement of initiative. Yet with the prevailing political philosophy of rewarding the unsuccessful and punishing the creators of our national abundance, there is no guarantee that we shall continue to be people of plenty. Washington is full of power-hungry mandarins and bureaucrats who distrust abundance, which gives people freedom, and who love scarcity and "zero growth," which give them power to assign, allocate, and control. If they ever win out, heaven help us! Americans do not know how to live with scarcity.

Copyright Acknowledgments

Index